ADVANCE PRAISE

Deserving of a wide audience, Stephen Reese is a gifted man whose pure heart is evident in every paragraph. His style is gentle and thorough (without being too professorial). I liked best his careful use of scriptural allusions and know of no Bible scholar who could have done it better.

—Bob Lively
Author, counselor, teacher-in-residence
at First Presbyterian Church of Austin

Steve Reese has given us a wise and heartfelt book, a thinking person's guide to matters spiritual that will strike a chord with thoughtful readers regardless of background or tradition.

—Tracy Dahlby
Author of *Allah's Torch: A Report from Behind the Scenes in Asia's War on Terror* and a former correspondent for *The Washington Post* and *Newsweek*

The writing has a wonderful humanity to it. Not many books on personal faith come out of the universities these days, but readers will be pleased, as I am, that the author decided to forget that tradition and give us this delightful and fulfilling volume.

—Wayne Danielson
Professor emeritus and former dean
College of Communication, University of Texas at Austin

D1473735

HOPE FOR THE THINKING CHRISTIAN
SEEKING A PATH OF FAITH THROUGH EVERYDAY LIFE

Smyth & Helwys Publishing, Inc.
6316 Peake Road
Macon, Georgia 31210-3960
1-800-747-3016
©2010 by Smyth & Helwys Publishing
All rights reserved.
Printed in the United States of America.

The paper used in this publication meets the minimum requirements of
American National Standard for Information Sciences—
Permanence of Paper for Printed Library Materials.
ANSI Z39.48–1984. (alk. paper)

Library of Congress Cataloging-in-Publication Data

Hope for the thinking Christian : seeking a path of faith through everyday life
by Stephen D. Reese. p. cm. Includes bibliographical references and index.
ISBN 978-1-57312-553-6 (pbk. : alk. paper)
1. Hope—Religious aspects—Christianity.
2. Thought and thinking—Religious aspects—Christianity.
I. Title. BV4638.R46 2010 234'.25—dc22 2010004642

STEPHEN REESE

HOPE

FOR THE
THINKING CHRISTIAN

SEEKING A PATH OF FAITH THROUGH EVERYDAY LIFE

To Carol, to Aaron and Daniel, and to Mom and Daddy

ACKNOWLEDGMENTS

I reflect later on the various influences on this book in the preface, but here I would like to give special thanks to a host of others.

Closest to home, I thank my family of encouragers. I'm especially grateful to my wife, Carol, who challenged me to go beyond my early personal writing efforts to create something bigger. She believed in the project, so I pursued it beyond preparing for her a homemade book as a Christmas gift to setting my sights on something more professional. My sons, Aaron and Daniel, were good sports about reading many of these reflections and being supportive (whether they'd read it or not). My brother, Vance, and sister, Eileen, lived some of these stories as participants, so I hope I've done justice to the history of our family and its importance to me. My mother-in-law and family nana, Marion, hasn't read it yet, but something tells me she'll like it. She's provided the same support and love I would have expected from my own mother, were she still here.

The vital community of faith at Oak Hill United Methodist Church has played a key role in my spiritual journey and thus in this project, inspiring and providing opportunities for sharing many of the reflections on which this volume is based. I've gotten to know some of its pastors more than others, but I would single out in thanks for their guidance and friendship the Revs. Barbara Ruth, John Wright, John Reynolds, and Val Sansing. Among the many uplifters at Oak Hill are my Stephen Minister colleagues, Methodist Men, and Emmaus community. A member of all three, my friend Jim Kester encouraged me until the last.

My agent-consultant, Kathleen Davis Niendorff, told me successful books in this genre have three things; I didn't have any of them, but she agreed to help me anyway. Anita Howard provided helpful editing; Bob Lively reassured me that some message was stirring in these chapters, as did Wayne Danielson and Bob Mann.

To these and all the others who read, listened, and shared your responses: bless you.

TABLE OF CONTENTS

PREFACE

People in the twenty-first century are spiritually challenged. With so many crosscutting cultural and social pressures, it takes dedicated work to build an honest faith. We live in a fast-moving, diverse society with distractions of mobility and affluence, both actual and desired. Families are mixed, blended, and far-flung. Often we are far from home, if we are even sure where "home" is. Many of us don't know where we'll be buried, and if we do there's no guarantee that our children will live nearby. Our faith may also feel dislocated. Our childhood faith, if we had one, now competes for validity with the many other religious traditions available in a global mix. We encounter others who don't believe as we do, often within our own extended families.

According to the 2008 "U.S. Religious Landscape Study," a survey of 35,000 adults carried out by the Pew Forum on Religion & Public Life, American faith shows a fluid, diverse pattern of belief in a competitive and ever-changing "marketplace." Protestants now make up just more than half (51 percent) of the adult population, with continued immigration likely to reduce this figure further. Among adults, 44 percent no longer follow the way they were reared: either they have switched affiliations, become affiliated when they weren't before, or dropped their affiliation altogether. The ranks of those unaffiliated, following no organized religion, have grown to 16 percent, with young people far more likely to be unaffiliated than older ones. If taking into account different Protestant denominations, a third of adults are intermarried (37 percent). At the same time, only 10 percent claim to be either agnostic, atheist, or "secular unaffiliated," a response meaning religion is not important in their lives. So the great majority
of Americans participate in this religious marketplace, but they are less likely to have a lifelong faith handed to them intact by their families—a trend that

likely will continue and oblige them to take a greater and more intentional role in shaping their own beliefs.

From these pressures, many may feel that they have only two real choices: seeking the absolutes of fundamentalism or rejecting faith altogether for a more secular, agnostic passivity. The polarization of American culture seems to push us toward one extreme or the other, and our stereotypes of the groups at both ends can get in the way of the search for an authentic spiritual identity. Both can create forms of idolatry. Among the New Atheists are figures like Richard Dawkins, best-selling author of *The God Delusion*, who go beyond defending scientific reasoning to reject religious belief altogether. Their antagonists, in turn, often call science the enemy of religion. Indeed, science in some quarters has become enshrined as its own form of religious, utopian belief system. This reinforces the regrettable framing of the conflict, as represented on one *Time* magazine cover, of "Science vs. God." The "God said it, I believe it, that settles it" absolutism can separate us from God just as surely as a rejection of God. The all-or-nothing offer of fundamentalism can turn away many who hunger for a spiritual connection.

A third way is more difficult to navigate but increasingly necessary. I want to explore this way and invite others to join me, especially the many seekers who would believe if only they could—and those who do believe but are not sure they should. That's where the vital conversation of faith lies. Judging from the surveys of public opinion on religion, most of us yearn at some level for meaning, for a faith that nourishes and sustains us through times of loss and fear, for a faith that brings greater joy: in short, for the abundant life. It is time to reject the impoverished debate that masquerades as a dialogue on religion so that we can get closer to seeing how an honest faith actually plays out in everyday modern life.

I use the term "thinking Christian" to refer to those who view the faith with a more open outlook, carefully and tactfully considering and respecting the faith paths of others. We need to confront our faith more directly, to think it through and be open to God in an individual, authentic, spiritual encounter. That doesn't mean making it an intellectual exercise or creating a cafeteria-style religion; it does mean holding to a spirit of tolerance with a sincere willingness to let God find us in God's own way, to surrender to God even before we figure it all out. This path will also require spiritual discipline on a daily basis. We must try to live with some sense of God's purpose as well as with what God expects of us.

From that awareness of divine purpose and expectation should come a desire to work out a faith understanding for ourselves. That's what I think Paul meant when he urged the Philippians to ". . . work out your own salvation with fear and trembling; for it is God who is at work in you, enabling you both to will and to work for his good pleasure" (Phil 2:12-13). That doesn't mean we cower before God as we desperately come up with our plan; rather, God plants something inside us that grabs us, and then urges us to better understand it. Paul expressed this in his simple, heart-felt declaration: "I want to *know* Christ" (Phil 3:10). Clergy and other faith professionals cannot do the work for us. We must do it for ourselves.

That's where I find myself. With the help of many spiritual guides along the way, I have wrestled with how to experience God more fully and to understand what God expects of me within an intellectually honest faith. That doesn't always fit the stereotypes of being "religious," but I'm not bothered by that. I suspect many people have the same yearnings I do. I wanted to write about not merely an introspective conversation with myself but about what I imagine is a larger dialogue with fellow travelers; I wanted to pose important questions that perhaps aren't asked often. Where does the thoughtful believer fit in the community of faith? How do we navigate between the false dichotomies of fundamentalism and anti-religious secularism? How can we reconcile the need to be tolerant of other believers while being passionate about our spiritual journeys? As I've wrestled with these questions through my life experiences, I want to show, not just tell—to reveal something deep inside and not just make it an intellectual exercise. My credibility in this area extends only as far as my ability to be authentic and to find something that resonates with others. I'm not an expert or a religious professional. I don't claim to have it all figured out, but I've seen how difficult the daily challenge of belief can be in my own life and for my friends. I was led to try to ponder it for myself. I explore the particular difficulty faced by professional men in making themselves vulnerable and being open about their faith and inner life. Of course, I intend the book to speak to women as well. I write out of my own experience, but these issues are common to almost all of us. The dialogue I initiate lies at the intersection of the societal and the personal, the theological and the devotional.

This book is a faith journey through everyday life, confronting the challenge of staying spiritually intentional in a demanding world of work and family. I want to do better at being a friend, a husband, a dad, a teacher, and a man. Though they don't comprise an exhaustive list, each chapter arises from a specific challenge I have faced and now choose to share with other seekers like me. I intend to explore the following general themes:

- Needing to understand what we believe about God in a diverse, often polarizing world
- Finding our individual spiritual identity and coming to terms with the meaning of "success"
- Integrating a faith experience with the often compartmentalized worlds of work and home
- Living intentionally through the daily demands of professional life
- Being honest about ourselves and confronting the limitations that may threaten our professional image
- Confronting anxieties about the future, especially the direction of the professional path
- Dealing with the loss of a parent or loved one
- Being a present and caring friend, especially when we find others in need
- Navigating the road of parenthood and being a loving support to a young person
- Searching for greater intimacy within a marriage
- Remaining faithful through suffering, including the vulnerability of illness, loss, and disappointment

I'm a college professor, and I tell my students that means I'm a professional learner. I think and learn—then I write and teach about what I've learned. Here I do the same, but this it's about that most intimate of zones, my personal spirituality. The chapters in this volume came about largely as talks at men's retreats and other gatherings at which I reflected on a particular spiritual principle and how it plays out in my life. So, in the process of writing this book, I tried to articulate something out of my experience, watch how it resonated with others, and reflect on why it seemed to make a connection. As often happens in the writing process, I've reread my work to see what I've tried to say to myself. It's an unusual "out of body" experience to read words that I no longer recall writing in exactly those ways. They have taken on a life of their own. Even though I may no longer face all the challenges I describe here, these reflections remind me that I did face them and that God has worked in my life to bring me to the present. I see a man I recognize and feel sympathy for him. Perhaps you will too.

A number of important influences have shaped my work. I'm grateful to writers such as Anne Lamott and Donald Miller, who have brought a fresh prose style and popularity to the Christian spirituality genre. They have helped loosen my sense of how to express my ideas as I try to avoid—not with complete success, I'm sure—the often stilted prose and jargon of my profession. Other more formal theological writers have also helped point the way for me, such as Parker Palmer and Richard Rohr. Austin writer, pastor, and counselor Bob Lively gave me encouragement and prompted me to expand my vision for this book toward a broader dialogue with other thinking Christians. Bishop John Shelby Spong has been particularly influential in helping me develop an intellectually compatible Christianity—including how to approach Scripture and better appreciate the powerful role of Judaism in undergirding and informing my faith. Coincidentally, his brother, the late Rev. Will Spong, challenged me as a pastoral counselor to grow at a critical time. Although many others have contributed to my spiritual formation, in recent years I single out the Rev. John Wright, who served as my pastor, spiritual adviser, and friend while at Oak Hill United Methodist Church in Austin. He taught me about grace and reminded me of the Wesleyan ideal: the joining of head and heart.

Men often have a hard time expressing their deepest feelings to their children. Caught up in the routine, we assume our kids already know how we feel, or we think sharing with them may embarrass them or us. But children want to know about their parents. I wish I could have been privy to more of my parents' interior lives. My dad wasn't the type to dwell on his, and my mom was my mom. We don't often think to ask these things growing up. But as I look back on my writing, I realize that I share a great deal about myself, more than perhaps I ever thought I might, and more than I often think I have. That being the case, I hope that my sons will be able to say they knew what was going on in their dad's life and heart. And beyond my own family, I trust that God will speak through my experience and reflections and encourage you in yours.

Stephen D. Reese
Austin, Texas

Chapter 1

HOPE FOR THE THINKING CHRISTIAN

Spiritual thinking means asking questions without easy answers and being content to let those questions rest in paradoxical mystery. Those kinds of questions, however, are often frustrating and disturbing, especially in a high-tech, advanced society with a bias toward action, productivity, and problem-solving. It's much more comforting to get right to the answers with religion—and to meet any challenges to those answers with redoubled convictions. That's why a fundamentalist world lies embedded within modern society where many find comfort in religious ideas that are believed forcefully and unquestioningly and who often wish to project those beliefs onto others in a universalizing sweep. That's the nature of fundamentalism: it says more about the way something is believed than about the beliefs themselves. The modern world is a frightening place, especially to millions who aren't able to adapt to it or who find their privileged place in the culture threatened by difference. Others on the outside looking in see in the modern the enemy of their traditional way of life. Fundamentalism—whether Islamic, Christian, Hindu, Jewish, or otherwise—has become stronger as a means of controlling the uncontrollable, as a backlash against change, and as a retreat into certainty, which unfortunately translates into division and clash of belief rather than community.

In American society, the role of religion in public life has shifted in recent years with a wider range of political groups, including liberals and progressives, using the language of faith and breaking the Right Wing's ability to claim a lock on Christian morality. But in a post-Bush America, fundamentalist belief is not going away; if anything, it is building. Political leaders, claiming that American institutions are under attack from secular humanist "culture warriors," stoke public anxieties. I've been inclined to ignore such hyperbolic rhetoric, but I don't think we can afford to do that. The conflict is no longer confined to the political arena. For fundamentalists, the church easily takes its place next to these other "revered institutions," and becomes part of a package of unquestioned belief that drives out authentic spirituality.

The disturbing documentary *Jesus Camp* tracks the experiences of middle-class Pentecostals who brought their kids to a special program for indoctrination, which included a speaker who had built a creationist museum and who claimed that dinosaurs lived with Adam and Eve. Anti-evolution advocates want their ideas represented in the science curriculum and have achieved some success by framing their approach with the more reasonable sounding "intelligent design," a view no longer marginalized as quaint backwoods dogmatism of the under-educated. It has taken hold at the center of the American culture. Thoughtful Christians should resist these tendencies, however; they should keep asking the questions that aren't easily answered and defend the space in their communities and spirits where we allow the mystery of God to live. Many thoughtful people don't find their questions answered by shouting the debate more loudly. Critical thinkers are turned off by simplistic beliefs that either never worked or don't work anymore. There must be a place for those people in the life of faith; they are the ones who know intuitively that the mysteries of the spirit can't have such easy answers.

I want to understand where that place is and to occupy it. I want to know how thoughtful people can find a spiritual home in a world of fundamentalism. Although religious terminology varies, I don't equate fundamentalism with evangelicalism, which broadly centers on the sacrifice of Jesus, the personal conversion experience of being "born again," and the important role of the Bible. Often in league with conservative politics, evangelicalism has come to include a more liberal strand associated with figures like former president Jimmy Carter and *Sojourners* magazine editor Jim Wallis; this has also been called a "cosmopolitan evangelicalism" that finds common cause with other progressive social policies. I use "fundamentalism" to refer to the more conservative version of Christianity but more broadly to a style of belief, a mindset within many religious traditions. Opposing this tendency, thinking Christians need to find a way of believing that both allows them to live in community and nourishes their inner spirits. They must be at home in their communities of faith and in their spirits, which ultimately means being at home with God. As a thoughtful person myself, I hope, I want to find that kind of home. Although I don't intend to write a book on theology or a diatribe against political or cultural groups with which I disagree, I do need to know what's going on in the world, including the fundamentalist drift in our culture, so I can make sense of my faith and the forces that threaten it.

Against this backdrop I struggle to understand my faith through my experience of everyday life. My beliefs are rooted in the Christian tradition, but I want to be a thoughtful Christian. I assume that regardless of one's faith tradition, we all want to be thoughtful about our spiritual practices while finding a way to be enthusiastic about them. The life of the spirit, after all, means letting go and not holding back, but we still need to find a way to live peacefully in community with others.

The thinking Christian faces difficult questions: How can we care for each other if we disagree? Do we need consensus of belief to have a community of faith? How can I honor the claims of Jesus of his own divinity while allowing room for those who don't? These days, such questions take on greater urgency because we are more likely to encounter people whose perspectives differ from those of our own religious tradition. Perhaps we're reluctant to bring up the subject for fear of offending them. Or maybe we feel obliged to defend a tradition to which we may ourselves only loosely subscribe. When we are immersed in a community that believes as we do, our individual practices recede into the background. We know that's just how it's done. But when we encounter difference, our particular ways of doing things become a source of potential conflict. When awareness of difference, of the "other," threatens the security of their inner identity, some people respond with redoubled enthusiasm for the correctness of their beliefs and draw sharper tribal lines. Others may conclude that certain ways of believing are not so important after all. Beliefs get compartmentalized or held loosely with a sense of detachment, making it more difficult for them to become ways of drawing closer to God. They lose their standing as means of grace in which to be immersed without reservation. Or we become so aware of our own convictions that we can't put aside that double-consciousness of spiritual identity—how we see that identity and how we think others see it. That sense of ironic detachment may make the whole thing seem merely arbitrary. I worry that the conversation of faith too closely resembles how the poet, W. B. Yeats, expressed it: "The best lack all conviction, while the worst are full of passionate intensity" (from "The Second Coming").

Within families, these differences cause particularly painful conflict or at least confusion. When family members change religious homes, observers may feel that those individuals have left the fold and are challenging the validity of long-standing beliefs. Tolerance may seem like avoiding whole-hearted loyalty to our beliefs. The boundaries of religion should never prevent the flow of love between individuals; yet, in our humanness, we are endlessly creative in using religion to block that flow. In divorce cases, for example, the number of conflicts over religion has increased. An article in the *New York Times* observed that when interfaith parents divorce or one changes a faith affiliation after the split, it causes friction. Judges, because they prefer not to take religious sides, often favor the parent who is more religiously engaged. At the center of a custody struggle between a man and his ex-wife who had become more fundamentalist, one child said about her dad, "Maybe he thinks her religion may be bad for me, but I think mainly he doesn't like my mom and is using that as an excuse." Such cases show how easy it is, even within families, to use religion to gain advantage over another.[1]

As I wrote these chapters, my brother told me he had decided—after a lifelong and deeply involved Christian experience—to become a Jew. He holds a doctorate of music in organ and church music, has been on staff at a number of congregations including a synagogue, and cared about matters of faith and issues of social justice long before I did. I knew he had thought it through and felt strongly about his decision, so I wrote to him saying how thankful I am that he found a new faith family that obviously loved and accepted him so warmly. I said I knew God was seeking him out in the way that was most pleasing to God, and he had responded accordingly. Nevertheless, even at my most tolerant, I couldn't help feeling a little unsettled, and I am certain that this situation went over more easily with our parents no longer living. I could imagine them wondering, "Where did we go wrong? What about all we did to bring you up in the church, all those years of Sunday school?" For a Jew who becomes Christian, I imagine adding to something; the "Judeo" becomes the "Judeo-Christian." But what about when the Judeo-Christian becomes "just" a Judeo: what happens to Jesus when Jesus has occupied such a prominent place for so long? My brother explained that he finds Judaism similar to Methodism in its emphasis on social justice, and I accept that he hasn't repudiated Jesus (or, more honestly, threatened my Jesus), but rather he has embraced a different part of his faith with greater emphasis.

At some point, my brother explained, he felt more at home with his Jewish congregational family, and for many years, he had no longer felt at home on the "continent of Christianity." He had been "at sea." My brother has always felt somewhat like an outsider to the culture in general—especially its more commercialized and militarized aspects—and I can't say I blame him. I'll let his journey be his to explain another day, but he's not the only one who no longer feels at home in the religious culture of his youth. Political leaders within my faith tradition have invoked Christianity for their own goals, devoting far more energy to waging preemptive war than to trying to live in community, as I thought we were called to do. The fundamentalist drift leads to irrelevant sideshows like the so-called "War on Christmas," where somehow the faith is considered under attack if retail clerks don't wish their customers "Merry Christmas." I hope my spirituality doesn't depend on my ability to hear Christmas carols at Wal-Mart, but this kind of polarizing rhetoric makes it tough to find a home for the spirit in community. Setting off to sea, leaving the familiar behind, can mean feeling adrift in other areas too. To attract new members, many churches go out of their way to seem different and more attractive than churches in which recruits grew up: informal worship, upbeat contemporary music instead of hymns, speakers in jeans who use PowerPoint illustrations, and Starbucks in the lobby of symbol-free sanctuaries. But for many people it's no use; they reject the faith journey altogether.

I imagine that these kinds of conversations happen more and more often, particularly in families where differences hit so close to home, assuming that we don't simply agree to ignore them and avoid disturbing the peace at family gatherings. As communities become more connected and cosmopolitan and traveling and migration become easier, we only increase the likelihood of such conversations. On a business trip to Dubai, I stopped in Cairo to visit my son Aaron, who, after a semester abroad as a junior, went there again after graduating from college to work on his Arabic. Sitting in my hotel room, I heard the call to prayer and sermons broadcast loudly from the mosque towers nearby.

Bismil-lah ar-Rahman ar-Raheem. Al-hamdu li-laahi rab il-alameen. Ar-rahman ir-raheem. Malaki yowm ad-deen. Iyaka nu'abudu wa 'iyaka nesta'een. Ehdina siraat al-mustaqeem. As-sirat alatheena in'amta alayhim wa ghayer al-maghdoobi alayhim wa la daaaleeen. Ameen.

When my son translated this frequent daily prayer for me, it felt familiar and
not so different from what I would pray.

> In the name of God, the Merciful, the Compassionate. Praise be to God, Lord
> of the worlds. The Merciful, the Compassionate. Master of the Day of
> Judgment. You alone do we worship, and You alone do we ask for help. Guide
> us upon the correct path, the path of those you have blessed and not that of
> those with whom you are angry. Amen.

My profession as an educator is not the only one that connects people
more globally—in my case, colleagues include Mormons, Hindus,
Buddhists, Opus Dei Catholics, Muslims, Bible-church and mega-church
"seekers," and other traditions they haven't yet told me about. They are all
part of those with whom I am called to live in community. We can easily
find our echo chambers filled with like-minded believers, but Christianity
originated at the crossroads of the world. Roman citizen Paul preached in
Athens, a city so diverse in belief that, to be on the safe side, an altar was
built to "the unknown God." Christianity, notwithstanding its
Americanization, has cosmopolitan roots.

Within this climate of difference, I keep coming back to one question:
Where do I fit in the Body of Christ? All who love God and want to know
God can find a place in the sense that I mean, even if they don't call themselves Christian. To me, Christ embodies all that God wants to do in human
lives and how God would have us lose ourselves in something bigger and live
more fully than we can out of our own power. When we come together in
love of God and each other, we join and *become* that body. However, the tolerance for difference often gives way to an exclusionary urge, the idea that
either one accepts Christ or—and this is the more generous characteriza-
tion—one is separated from God. In my life, I experience the grace of God
through following Christ, and I'm part of a faith culture and participate in a
community for which Christ has become the symbolic embodiment of unity
with God. Still, I want to find a place in the Body of Christ that doesn't
mean rejecting others or prematurely closing off other ways of experiencing
God. We can love each other in spite of religious differences, for there is a
spark of the divine in each of us. Love works better if we focus on that spark.

The Apostle Paul was the most enthusiastic missionary for Jesus in the
Bible, but even Paul's Christian theology began with the grace of God. He
was clear about what mattered most, arguing that in Christ "the only thing
that counts is faith working through love" (Gal 4:6). In the Christ I know, as

Paul says, ". . . all things hold together . . . . For in him all the fullness of God was pleased to dwell" (Col 1:17-19). When we look at Christ we see God, and to the extent that we can take on the spirit of Christ, lose ourselves in God, and become one with the Father as Christ said he was, then we know God, we fellowship with God, and life "works." Life holds together. As central as Christ was to Paul, he saw beyond Christ to what Christ represented.

In my commuting time in the car, I scan the radio for something interesting. Sometimes that includes religious broadcasters, with whom I inevitably part ways theologically. I disagree with the politics and narrow-mindedness of many of them, including psychologist and Republican-booster James Dobson, but I sometimes find something to like in his "Focus on the Family." Where else on the radio will I find conversations about love in families? For many years, I've listened to the "In Touch" ministries program with Charles Stanley, a Baptist preacher in Atlanta, the former head of the Southern Baptist Convention, and a one-man cottage industry in broadcasting and publishing. I am occasionally repelled by his right-wing politics and somewhat exclusionary theology, but vast numbers are drawn to his sermons on practical issues of daily living—including me. Like them, I'm animated by the same desire to find something holy in everyday life, and I can usually find a message, even if I don't agree with the entire platform. I sympathize with parents who want to home school their kids out of fear of the secular culture. There's a lot to fear. The answer, however, is not a fearful retreat behind tribal lines into more insulated certainty and freedom from difference. While still appreciating the yearning for something more out of life that drives many of my fundamentalist neighbors, I believe there's another way.

Thoughtful Christians must make use of reason to understand their faith, but we ultimately can't use logic to argue God into or out of existence, though many people try. Equating God with our logical capabilities makes God something or nothing on the basis of our personal criteria. The life of faith has to start with a connection with something beyond our human limits of reason. As the power in the universe greater than myself, a loving God continually woos me, desiring to lift me outside myself into the abundant life. I can't logically prove that God is doing that; I can only be aware of that presence as it works itself out in my life, and I can become more keenly aware of the moments when I feel God's presence most deeply. I desire to enter into a realm beyond myself, as I think many do, to have a tantalizing awareness of a world beyond my material existence. Connecting with that larger world of spirit requires that we step outside our boxes of reasoning, also known as a "taking a leap of faith." Paul couldn't start with his own reasoning and work toward God because, until his Damascus road conversion, his initial beliefs got in the way of the full experience of God that he eventually found in Christ. I think Paul, deeply intelligent and knowledgeable, took a leap of faith, and once he opened the door to God's power in his life he began to work it out in every other respect.

Many attempt to reason God into existence by "fundamentalizing" certain key assumptions about who God is and what God has decided to do, and they hold fast to their ways of defining God. Belief itself becomes God, stopping short of the true "ultimate." In his published lectures, *Runaway World: How Globalization Is Reshaping Our Lives*, sociologist Anthony Giddens expands the meaning of fundamentalism beyond specific religious connotation to refer to how "the truth of beliefs is defended or asserted."[2] It is truth that comes from authority that often results in "a refusal of dialogue in a world whose peace and continuity depend on it."[3] The Bible becomes the fixed word, as though it were transmitted whole at one moment rather than evolving over centuries out of great cultural complexity; it speaks for itself rather than serving as a means through which God speaks to us. Beginning with certain "inerrant" Scriptures provides a framework through which "Bible-believing" Christians discern God's ways and intentions—and the means one must use to find God. This makes sense if one is able to assume complete biblical inerrancy, that is, divinely inspired literalness. The desire to support biblical truths leads many to insert this system of belief into realms where it doesn't belong, such as science. However, the system of scientific reason, regardless of where it leads, can never threaten the thinking Christian and the life of the spirit. Thus, people should not corrupt science in order to have it support some concept of God.

God becomes real in many ways. Some people find God in the context of symbols and practices or through certain vocabulary and images. Such practices were transmitted to me through the Christian church and through songs and narratives and myths and memories and, of course, the people who have become a part of my faith experience. God speaks to me through my lived experience, including the structure of my religious life. That doesn't make those structures incorrect or suspect because they speak more strongly to my faith community, but neither does it make them the only truth. An accident of birth doesn't privilege my cultural position; finding my home there simply privileges it for me.

However, starting from a position of certainty in what we ourselves have helped create corrupts the structures of belief that intend to bring us to God. It enshrines them so that they become a kind of god in themselves that only we possess and to which others must aspire. Like any human practice, their original purpose is easily turned upside down. We are rule-bound creatures, like the Pharisees whom Jesus criticized for being too wrapped up in the letter of the law and like pre-Damascus Paul who tried hard to excel in following the regulations. The Spirit is forgotten. The rule becomes the god rather than the means to a larger goal.

I attended a debate not long ago between Marvin Olasky (a conservative colleague and editor of an evangelical weekly magazine) and polemical author Christopher Hitchens. It was part of a tour to promote Hitchens's book, *God Is Not Great: Why Religion Poisons Everything.*[4] The pairing of these two frustrated me; the discussion was polarized between two unattractive extremes. Are these my only choices? Of course not, although they are often presented that way. God is neither refuted because people have done terrible things in God's name, as Hitchens claimed, nor is God God because people do good things in his name, as Olasky reported, citing numerous examples of Christians doing good deeds. The existence of God fortunately does not rest on the kinds of things—good or bad—people do on God's behalf. One of Hitchens's anti-religion arguments is that it doesn't make sense that a loving God folded his arms for thousands of years before finally providing Jesus to bring salvation. Indeed, this doesn't make sense if we think God acts on a particular human schedule, arbitrarily withholding grace until the opportune time. But if Jesus becomes God for us, then Jesus is God trying to reach us in a way that a significant number of people, on their own human schedule, can finally "get." What God is able to do depends greatly on our openness to God's movement.

Thinking Christians who encounter fundamentalism inevitably disagree with the exclusivity principle, which results from the literalist belief in Scripture and a doctrine that is both hard to defend on logical grounds and leaves little room for the mysterious paradox of faith. The more tightly one holds the conviction that Jesus is the true way to salvation, the more likely that way excludes others who don't agree. If Jesus is the only way, then what happens to babies who die before they accept Christ? What about people who live in remote jungle villages or in China (or in some other predominantly non-Christian country) who may never hear the gospel? Even open-minded Christians deal with this nagging question that they can never quite resolve.

Of course, when pressed, the more generous of the exclusivity believers offer an escape clause: God decides who has received a fair opportunity to hear the gospel and gives them a break if they haven't. Alternatively, some suggest the "state of innocence" provision: God has a certain cut-off age, known only to God, before which it isn't fair to exclude unbelievers who die prematurely. So the claim is that God gets to decide, but those who use the language of exclusion and inclusion imply that they actually decide and have decided (or at least know how the decision comes out). Thus, they can conclude that they believe the "right" things. This theology begins to fail, however, once they think more deeply about it, especially if they care for the people they fear may be doomed.

I wish to avoid a prolonged theological argument, but I've thought for a long time about something that helps me make sense of these questions. I believe the Bible is capable of becoming the word of God for us; I find the spark of divine inspiration in these writings, no matter how long they took to assemble and codify. Rather than viewing Scripture as the literal words God spoke, I read in them God's invitation to each of us. Others believe the Bible contains the word of God, and indeed, more pointedly, that it *is* the word of God. Some find great comfort in the archaeological discoveries that corroborate Bible stories (an ancient chariot wheel discovered in the Red Sea, for example, that some say proves the exodus story), while others want to develop a whole system of pseudo-science to support a biblically oriented explanation of human development. In the political arena, some think the specific structures of the religion itself should dominate the larger society: Bethlehem nativity scenes in the town square, the Ten Commandments in every courthouse, and carols played in the stores in December. These two perspectives are often reduced to the simplistic labels of, respectively, left vs. right; or "secular humanists/moral relativists" vs. traditional values/"Bible-believers." I feel that the thinking believer, while accepting the guiding role of faith in inner and public life, must go with a more open mindset that allows for more possibilities. There, we can find a deeply experienced, intimate relationship with God without narrow-minded theological and political baggage.

Some might call my theology one of "many paths to God," but that seems like some kind of postmodern, everything-is-relative copout. Isn't there a way, after all, to know the best path, a better place to stand than the ground of vague ecumenicalism? Perhaps not. In the paradox of faith, being "certain" doesn't work the same as in other areas of human experience. I remember the bumper sticker I read on a car near my office: "Surround yourself with those who seek God; flee those who claim they've found him." I like that one. As Paul told the Corinthians, "Anyone who claims to know something does not yet have the necessary knowledge" (1 Cor 8:12). Jesus himself cautioned against certitude, telling the Pharisees, "But now that you say, 'We see,' your sin remains" (John 9:41). The most passionate advocates of Christian faith are willing to rest in an open way of thinking about God. As John Wesley said, "Never dream of forcing men into the ways of God. Think yourself, and let think."[5] There is liberty in Christ, but that freedom is too often forgotten and short-circuited by the fundamentalist impulse.

I think it's important to make the distinction between two separate dimensions: "how" we believe and the quality of the inner spiritual life. One doesn't necessarily go with the other. Having an openness of thought about religious practice doesn't mean one can't have a dynamic spiritual life. Personal spirituality can be minimal, superficial, or nonexistent, even for those who are active in their religion. Among the fundamentalists, no doubt many are passionate about their inner spiritual lives, but this need not necessarily be the case. Although the believing mindset, the "how," may have little to do with the interior spirit, one might be tempted to take someone's passion for belief as evidence of that person's intimate relationship with God—to assume one is necessary to get the other. Many people are unwilling to make that bargain. Others are willing but find the belief system unable to deliver on its promise for a rewarding spiritual life. Moreover, the fundamentalist association with closed-mindedness and the political right may block people from engaging a faith tradition at all, hindering the search for a rewarding inner spiritual life before it even begins.

The open style of belief has its own impediments to nurturing the spirit. Indeed, openness to other traditions may paradoxically inhibit one entering fully into his or her own. I went to Las Vegas for the first time in the early 1980s for a conference at Caesar's Palace, still for me the iconic Vegas strip hotel. This was before the city became a more family-friendly, adult Disney World and still had a slightly seedy, underworld, Frank Sinatra "rat pack" image. Everything about it fascinated me: the moving sidewalks at Caesar's leading in from the street, which drew visitors from the sidewalk periphery past the fountains and faux classical decor to the casino (the sidewalks only went one direction, so you had to walk back if you wanted to leave) and into the windowless zones of slot machines and gambling tables. The controlled velvet rope access to the more exclusive baccarat tables created an atmosphere of regulated danger and risk. I noticed that there wasn't a clock in sight, and I wondered if it were true that they piped oxygen into the casino to keep the players awake. But during my few days there, I didn't feel the need to gamble more than a few bucks, and that was at a cheaper place down the road. I was simply intrigued by the whole scene, a sociological voyeur watching others play the game while I stood by.

I've returned a few times, but my reluctance to gamble any real money means I don't fully get into the spirit of the place. The point of going to a casino is to gamble, to let go of something valuable, to risk, and until you do you'll always be a spectator. Many folks doubtless feel that way about church—enjoying the scene, happy to take the kids, but reluctant to get into the spirit of the place. For an intellectual, it's easy to detach and have a sort of out-of-body experience, watching yourself "do church." While I support thinking faith through, we can think so much about it that we leave no room for the Spirit to take hold. We can be so hyper-aware of the many paths that we fail to follow any of them. Compartmentalizing faith marginalizes the spiritual experience—making it just another activity to check off in a busy schedule. Only with a fuller, all-embracing willingness to see the spiritual in everyday life can we make faith a deeply felt and immersive experience. Only then can the Gospels become the idea into which all other ideas fit—a way of thinking that brings understanding to everything else.

I want my place in the Body of Christ to lie in the space where an open style of belief joins with an immersive inner spiritual life. That is, I seek the place within these intersecting dimensions where I can be passionate about my inner spiritual life and still open and tolerant about faith within a community of diverse believers. I don't think that's a contradiction. I want to have passion for God within my life, yet remain at the place where openness to human structures on the outside allows room for the mysterious paradox of faith on the inside.

This kind of thinking takes intentional work, but it's available to anyone who wishes to try. However, there's a difference between thinking about faith and living faith. After we think about it, we need to give way to the Spirit. In the chapters that follow, I want to show—not merely tell—how I experience the spiritual as real life. I'm mindful of Richard Rohr's warning that "We do not think ourselves into new ways of living. We live ourselves into new ways of living."[6] In explaining my lived experience, I hope to demonstrate that there's something worth searching for. I hope to show that an immersive Christian experience can join an open framework of religious belief.

Mother Teresa has the unapproachable status that we give to saints we believe are in no way like us. She is a deserving model who lived and worked with the destitute poor, ministering to those most of us prefer to ignore. For me, her letters, which only came to light after her death and against her wishes, are the most powerful testimonials to her faith. They are honest about her interior struggle of doubt and her perception at times that God had abandoned her. Mother Teresa's confession enhanced her credibility because we all have such struggles; even saints are not immune from them. Hers was a real, lived struggle—not only an intellectual, theological debate. Even so, she continued to seek God and serve God through and in spite of those periods when she didn't always feel God's presence. That's the best any of us can do.

When my brother joined the tribe of Judaism, he shared the following prayer at his *D'var* ceremony. It expresses the questioning and the stopping just short of answers, the resting in mystery that we are called to do:

My Lord God, I have no idea where I am going. I do not see the road ahead of me. I cannot know for certain where it will end. Nor do I really know myself, and the fact that I think I am following your will does not mean that I am actually doing so. But I believe that the desire to please you does in fact please you and I hope that I have that desire in all that I am doing. And I know that if I do this, you will lead me by the right road although I may know nothing about it. Therefore will I trust you always though I may seem to be lost and in the shadow of death. I will not fear, for you are ever with me and you will never leave me to face my perils alone.[7]

I have a feeling that the author of that prayer, Thomas Merton, wouldn't feel much at home in many Christian communities, although he was a Trappist monk. They might insist on asking him whether he had accepted Jesus as his personal Savior, or whether he knew he was in the "Lamb's book of life," secure in his eternal salvation. But it seems Merton found that inner spirit in his questioning of the mystery of God, without the encumbrances of fundamentalizing structures.

I am convinced there is hope. We need not check our critical faculties at the door in order to immerse ourselves in a faith experience that allows us to grow. We are at a crossroads in American society, and we must resist having the life of faith corrupted by intolerance and anti-intellectualism. However, together with the fundamentalists of the world, we are subject to the same larger forces of cultural alienation and dehumanization. We all have this in common, and we all have much work to do on ourselves. Like others, I yearn for many things that will always be out of reach, but the life of the spirit is an infinite world of possibility; by the grace of God, it is always as close at hand as we wish it to be. Each of us needs to find and strengthen the spiritual in our lives, while finding ways to live authentically and peacefully in community. As more of us take that task seriously and thoughtfully, we are more likely to have a healthy society full of people with thriving, rich, and sustaining spiritual lives. This is the hope for the thinking Christian today.

Notes

1. Neela Banerjee, "Religion Joins Custody Cases, to Judges' Unease," *New York Times*, 18 February 2008, p. 18.

2. Anthony Giddens, *Runaway World: How Globalization Is Reshaping Our Lives* (New York: Routledge, 2003) 67.

3. Ibid.

4. Christopher Hitchens, *God Is Not Great: Why Religion Poisons Everything* (New York: Twelve, 2007).

5. John Wesley, *Sermons on Several Occasions* (New York: Land & Scott, 1851) 336.

6. Richard Rohr, *Everything Belongs: The Gift of Contemplative Prayer* (New York: Crossroad Pub., 2003) 19.

7. Thomas Merton, *Thoughts in Solitude* (New York: Farrar, Straus & Cudahy, 1958) 79.

Chapter 2

GETTING SERIOUS ABOUT FAITH

. . . but he said to me, "My grace is sufficient for you, for power is made perfect in weakness." So, I will boast all the more gladly of my weaknesses, so that the power of Christ may dwell in me . . . for whenever I am weak, then I am strong. (2 Corinthians 12:9-10)

Most people, whether fully conscious of it or not, reach a point where they want more out of life. For many, that leads to the search for meaning in deeper spiritual awareness. Why is it so difficult to satisfy that yearning and truly live a faith journey—and to do it "faithfully" as a daily discipline? Certainly, there's no shortage of advice. Bookstores offer upbeat, formula-based messages, often from leaders of television or mega-church ministries. Then there are deeper reflections of those who have made a "profession" of being spiritual, who may retreat for years of service, contemplation, and writing. In both cases, however, the message is often inaccessible to the average reader who must confront the daily secular grind. A formula approach is often simplistic, superficial, too unrealistic, or phony. Discouragement sets in if the first steps don't work, and those books end up stacked on dusty shelves. Readers of more contemplative works may conclude that this lifestyle can't work for them unless they drop out of their regular lives to go sit on a mountaintop somewhere, taking time for extended study or spiritual good deeds.

In other words, there many people just like me with a busy life and a full-time job. I'm not a professional theologian, spiritual thinker, or counselor. I do, however, want the "something more" out of life: to live a disciplined faith that takes me out of myself, to be able to live for something beyond my own narrow limits, to know God, and to let God use me for a higher purpose. It's easier said than done. In the first place, I'm not supposed to take faith, particularly Christianity, that seriously—much less write about it. I'm a man, a liberal, a college professor with multiple degrees, a husband in an interfaith marriage—all characteristics not usually associated with religiosity.

For a guy, faith means church, and church is associated with the feminine. David Murrow even wrote a book called *Why Men Hate Going to Church*, arguing that men don't want to go to school on Sunday after working all week.[1] Women are more involved in churches; much of the devotional literature is clearly written for women, beautifully packaged and targeting issues of home and family. Many men go along with religious practice because it's expected of them. It's part of being a respectable member of the community, being a parent, doing something for the kids. But they never get too serious about it, much less introspective.

My grandfather went to church every other Sunday. If our visit to my grandparents' home in West Tennessee fell on a Sunday, we dressed up to go to the Raleigh Baptist Church, beloved by my grandmother, who was a charter member. If it wasn't his Sunday to go to church, my granddaddy might just rock on the front porch instead. My own dad said the same mealtime prayer every evening: "Our gracious heavenly Father, we're thankful to thee for this day and for the blessings that thou hast given us. [pause] Amen." It sounded official with the "thou" and "hast," and it never deviated in word or inflection. If some of us came late to the table, he went ahead and said the blessing so he could start eating. Of course, it was just a little prayer before supper, but I suppose in my mind it seemed more like an incantation than a prayer that required any thought. Looking back, I don't question the sincerity of either man. Most guys didn't pray out loud and off the cuff, and the content of our family theology was never a topic of conversation. In that respect, both my grandfather and father were typical of other men of their eras and backgrounds.

Where I grew up, on the Appalachian side of Tennessee, the high Methodist church I attended was an outpost of theological reserve in an otherwise fundamentalist area. The ministers led worship with an elegant speaking style, crafting their phrases with a formality that fit the sanctuary's tall ceiling and formal arches. Those who truly got excited about their spiritual lives were considered "holy rollers" and attended the Pentecostal back-road congregations where any number of bizarre behaviors were said to occur. On the radio, I heard country preachers who, for reasons never clear to me, punctuated their phrases with a guttural exclamation: "Haa!" As in, "And Jesus . . . Haa! . . . said to the devil . . . Haa!" These people were a regular source of amusement mixed with fascination, and I passed many a long drive tuning them in at night on AM radio. In this low-tech sermonizing, which was often repackaged for Sunday morning worship, the volume of the "Amen corner" and occasional background shrieks from the congregation revealed the size of the church. Early televangelists were available on pre-cable television, including faith healers like "The Earnest Angley Miracle Crusade [as in Crusaaay-daa!]." The backwoods sermons seemed more genuine than the television programs, but in either case, their black-and-white theology left no room for doubt about how to get to heaven. The "Jesus saves" billboards on the highway to the nearby Great Smokey Mountains were a regular reminder of the local religion. Although I always had a keen sociological interest in these things, getting too worked up about religion was suspect. From the perspective of my stiff-upper-lip church home, such excitement was associated with the lower forms of spiritual life in the region.

As politics go, I fall on the left side of the spectrum, and liberals aren't supposed to be overtly religious. We're what the fundamentalists call "secular humanists," who, if we have a faith life at all, prefer either to hide it from view or to clearly separate it from public lives. It's considered embarrassing to talk about spirituality if you're on the left, and that is doubly true for academics. College professors are unfairly painted as anti-religion, though the life of the mind often seems to conflict with the life of the spirit. When I went to graduate school at the solidly liberal University of Wisconsin, I attended church from time to time. I thought it was something I should do, but it certainly was not a priority, nor did it appear so for my professors and fellow students. The idea of a faith life never came up. When I became a professor, I found to my surprise that a respected colleague in my department was a regular churchgoer. He even taught a Sunday school class! It didn't fit my image of him, a man at the top of our profession; I obviously based this perception on my—partly confirmed—stereotype of academia. Not long afterward, I heard another nationally reputed colleague reveal that he was a member of a local Baptist church. I admit I found it surprising, even though he mentioned it in the context of his talk at a campus research conference about religion and the media. Studying religion sat in uneasy proximity to being religious. Lately, I've been forced to rethink the idea that the "soft" world of faith doesn't go with the tough intellectualism I once thought I needed to get to the top.

Then there's the issue of my mixed-faith marriage to a Jew, something my early Tennessee upbringing would not have predicted. At age eight, I heard reports from the other kids about the only Jew in our school. I wasn't sure what shocked me more: that he didn't believe in Jesus or that he was required to attend "church" school on Saturdays! Both seemed equally abhorrent. Soon after, a family friend converted to Judaism when she married, and I wondered if she gave up the promise of eternal life that I was taught was the privilege of Christians. How would her parents feel about that? Now, some may wonder how it is possible for me to take a Christian faith seriously and yet enter into a marriage with a "nonbeliever." In the view of many, one religion would seem to exclude the other.

When I first thought about sharing my reflections on faith, I wasn't sure I was qualified. After all, I'm not supposed to take this search seriously, much less write a book about it. Aren't there others with more dramatic stories? The cliché is that one can't write about the spiritual life without the life-shattering experience of hitting rock bottom followed by a specific salvation experience. Certainly, personal crises often pave the way for dramatic experiences of healing faith by destroying our sense of strength. The recovery movement provides a powerful model for the grace of God, but unfortunately, it can seem that the quality of the newfound faith is only as good as the utter ruin of the life that led up to it. What about someone like me? I'm relatively well adjusted, and my life is unbroken by addiction or loss of health, job, or relationships. I hope it remains so.

Nevertheless, I'm convinced that everyone is in some kind of crisis, including the more existential kind that happens when we confront the limits of our everyday lives with the desire for something more. I share the experience of that crisis with my friends, coworkers, and the hundreds of other people I encounter every week. The way forward, however, is less clearly mapped for this kind of "recovery." I want to confront this everyday spiritual challenge, and for that I'm well qualified. I'm convinced there are many like me who want something more out of life but can't picture themselves taking the spiritual life seriously.

Why is it so difficult to make the "faith journey" a central part of one's life? Perhaps we think we must set aside a special time for "religious work," and outside of those times the "everydayness" of our routines makes it tough to be intentional about faith. But spirituality is not merely a part of life: it's a *way* of life. It's life itself. In pleading with the Israelites to take their relation-ship with God seriously, Moses urged them to absorb the laws so completely that he could say, "These instructions are not mere words—they are your life" (Deut 32:47). How much more joyful and satisfying life would be if we could become so full of the words God speaks to us that they would fill every space in our lives? For me, that means intentionally pursuing a faith experi-ence through the entire range of my life—family, work, and relationships—lifting everyday life up to where I more readily see God's hand at work. God speaks to me most strongly through the Christian tradi-tion, and its fundamental message for me is that God's power is made perfect in weakness. The Apostle Paul said, "Therefore, I will most gladly boast all the more about my weaknesses, so that Christ's power may reside in me" (2 Cor 12:9).

Getting serious about faith means getting ready, becoming open, and being available to something outside ourselves. To the extent that we render ourselves weak enough to be vulnerable, give up being strong on our own terms, and open ourselves to the loving power of God, we become free to live more fully and express that loving power to others. Why is this so difficult? Like my act of turning these writings loose and making them public beyond a small group of family and friends, opening myself to God exposes my inner life, something many of us go to great lengths to conceal. We all wrestle with this basic tension. We deeply desire intimate loving relationships, to be known fully by at least one person. Yet we fear allowing even that one person to know us for who we truly are. We want to be known on our own terms, orchestrating them to reveal only our strengths. We are not strong enough to acknowledge our true weaknesses.

For men, especially, revealing weakness often requires what C. S. Lewis called a "blessed defeat," a moment in life when we are rendered weak enough to finally give up to God.[2] I'm convinced that God has chipped away at me for a long time with a number of "born-again" experiences, but the most recent and powerful one came about through a series of moments when I confronted myself in midlife and faced who I truly am. I stopped trying to reason out God as merely another extracurricular activity. I faced a painful gap between where I was and where and who I wanted to be. Closing that gap meant accepting reality and trusting God's power to heal the breach. I also had to trust my family and intimate friends with an honest picture of myself. Finally, I surrendered and let God fully catch up to me. You can call that a born-again experience if you like, but regardless of the label, it was a new realization of how God has wooed me for a long time. Since then, I've grown more willing to risk seeming, in Paul's words, "foolish," and more confident that acknowledging weakness is the best way to demonstrate real strength. I continue to work on that risking and surrendering.

Why is it, then, that people like me are not supposed to take faith seriously? I wonder if we think we're expected to have a greater certainty about our beliefs than we feel. Unless we can jump in with both feet, we may be afraid to stick even a toe into the water. But if I understand Paul's principle, faith invites me to enter into the uncertain, to put aside my strength of certitude and become more open to God. A little religious knowledge goes a long way with some people, cementing their convictions in place, but I am willing for greater learning to bring me the paradoxical invitation to greater mystery. As Barbara Brown Taylor says in her book, *Leaving Church*, she learned to prize holy ignorance more than religious certainty.[3]

So much faith rhetoric these days takes a "strong" exclusionary and dualistic emphasis. Either you are saved or you are lost. My own Protestant upbringing put the choice less starkly. When we were kids, my younger brother wanted to hear Billy Graham when his "Crusade" came to our town. My parents couldn't easily oppose the idea, but they still felt uneasy about how we might respond to the "altar call." That, of course, was the inevitable moment at the end of the rally when all were invited to make a commitment for Christ—to publicly make their way down the steps of the vast football stadium to the area in front of the platform. Because my brother was a deeply sensitive young man, I think my parents imagined him an easy target for that kind of appeal. As a child, one night he closed the bedroom door and refused to let our parents hear his bedtime prayer. He had taken Matthew to heart, in which Jesus said, "Enter thy closet . . . and shut thy door," praying to the Father in secret. Perhaps our parents wondered how a conversion experience might disrupt our family's existing faith routine.

I will return later to this strand of American faith, so familiar to me in my upbringing and in my interior faith conversation. Many of my young friends were involved in evangelical groups, including a Catholic high school friend who treated me to my first beer, a 16-ounce "tall boy" from the drive-up window. But that was before his conversion experience led him to ditch his music collection, which he decided was a bad influence. Sincere as they were, those friends always made me uncomfortable in a way I couldn't explain. If I were a Christian, which as a church member I figured I must be, then where was my "testimony" and my personal moment when I accepted

Christ once and for all? I couldn't bring myself to buy fully into the "four spiritual laws" plan for salvation, clearly diagrammed on the brochures passed around by campus evangelical groups.[4] Jesus did tell his followers they must be "born again," but in my adulthood I see how easily we reduce that command to a simple mantra. In doing so, we risk limiting God to a responder to a magic incantation. It is possible to idolize some conception of God and forget that God is larger than our understanding of God. A certainty of beliefs can close us to God as surely as the absence of belief. Faith means being willing to open myself to God and to acknowledge honestly that there are questions to which I will never know the answers. Because everything we know about God is filtered through our human understandings, we cannot lift ourselves out of that framework and stand apart from it. That's where God is. As the fundamentalist approach to Christianity gains the spotlight in American society, I return to my original question: Where do people like me fit?

We often don't fit into organized religion. Tolerance in a faith community brings openness, but it also can bring tension and interpersonal friction as members try to find common ground. Methodism is the religion of my parents, and its practices are familiar and comfortable to me. I remain in that denomination because of its relatively open-minded perspective. I suppose I tend away from making a fetish of certainty through, if nothing else, my marriage. My wife, Carol, grew up in a predominantly Jewish neighborhood in Boston, where her faith practices were more the rule than the exception. Public schools observed Jewish holidays. Years earlier, her mother had considered marrying a Christian, but the idea made her father (Carol's grandfather) cry and was abandoned. Marriages can bring conflicting religious values to the foreground, but fortunately our own interfaith plan didn't cause family tears. We held our wedding in a building that was once a synagogue and a Methodist church, officiated by a Methodist minister who felt comfortable helping us craft a mutually agreeable ceremony. Borrowing from the Jewish tradition, I crushed the ceremonial glass underfoot at the end. We've come a long way since the first time my wife accompanied me to church. Exploiting her unfamiliarity with our particular rituals, I teased her by periodically clubbing my chest with my fist, like a Roman soldier's salute, and performing a number of other elaborate pseudo-sacred hand gestures, seeing if I could get her to follow suit. Although she and I have found many points of religious overlap, I am still obliged to think through exactly why I believe what I do. What are the essentials of my belief, and what is only the accumulation of tradition and cultural happenstance? Didn't Jesus say no one comes to the Father except through him (John 14:6)? In the past, I didn't want to examine that verse too closely. How could I think I'm "saved" and my wife is not? Even if I thought that, it would be tough to explain it to our children. ("I hate to tell you this, boys, but your mom's going straight to hell.")

A relationship like mine means that even in the most intimate zone of the family, I can't surround myself with others who believe just as I do. The Hanukkah candles and manger scene compete for space on our dining room table every December. I'm sure others have differing religious opinions within their families, and the holidays in particular can bring conflicts even within homes that share the same basic theology. Those differences take on a more explicit quality when different faith traditions are there from the beginning. Otherwise, I think it's easier simply to let many beliefs go unquestioned. When one or both partners are apathetic toward faith, there need be no conflict.

Without being any less serious about faith, I've found that I can live with someone who does not embrace the full range of my own beliefs (and vice versa for my wife). Certainly, with our children we have both needed to be prepared to articulate a defensible faith that we can pass along to them. I'm not saying we have talked it all through. We simply hold some beliefs in theological tension. I often wonder how many perfectly polite young people sit in my wife's middle-school classroom during the week and on Sunday hear a message that explicitly consigns them to heaven and not her. As for me, I'm ultimately willing to accept that the strongest response I can make theologically is often a weak but strangely satisfying one: "I don't know." As the man said to Jesus, "I believe, help thou my unbelief" (Mark 9:24). In place of strong certainty, I am willing to find refuge in a "weak" but honest acceptance of God's mystery.

As religious groups align themselves with political interests, especially on the right, it seems that liberals like me are left out. But "liberal" has become an easy label to apply to anyone who doesn't agree with the prevailing drift, whether politically or theologically. I resist being labeled in the simplistic way that term is often used. It's not difficult for people to equate faith with stronger political certainties, to make faith synonymous with a moral position. To be a Christian means, in some circles and in many churches, being told to support a specific political party or candidate. As a self-confessed political liberal, I resent being defined by what passes these days for the

"Christian" position. That means I often feel like an outsider in much of the current evangelical political conversation, and I run the risk of others assuming I believe things I don't. I think, however, if by "liberal" one means theological openness, then I have plenty of company. When former President Bush says, "God speaks through me," he gets it wrong. It's all right to desire that God would speak through us, but the moment we conclude that God has, and that we speak for God, we take on an arrogance that runs counter to Paul's principle. Maybe I don't fit politically, but my politics don't equal my faith, even if they are guided by it. I don't want to make an idol of a belief and assert that God has dictated one position or another, left or right. Faith should lead us constantly to measure our entire range of political beliefs against a prophetic standard.

Finally, there's the issue of my professional life. How does a faith life fit with what I do? Often it doesn't. I am fortunate to have a good education and a prestigious job, so I have a stake in looking like an expert. Maybe that's why academics don't write much devotional literature. The worlds of reason and faith are traditionally uneasy partners, but there is a more personal reason why faith and academia don't mix. Writing on the subject of faith leads me to step outside my area of expertise. Given the hyper-competitive world of university life, my job by its nature is tied to appearances—of seeming competent, smart, and in control. For someone like me, it can be difficult to become more spiritually open, to take on the kind of weakness Paul says God can better use. At stake are an ego and an image painstakingly constructed over the years. A crisis hasn't necessarily forced the issue and crumbled the wall that separates my inner and outer lives. But John Wesley's encouragement that the heart and mind should be reunited in the believer has guided me to try reconciling the two.[5]

So, I do take living the Christian life seriously, but that also means dealing with social categories that don't always fit the mold and figuring out how I fit. But we must all do that. The geographical and psychological mobility of modern life causes our defining affiliations to pile up and mix together. As recent surveys showed, fewer of us come to our faith experience with the same kind of demographic certainty that was often the case in simpler times, when people followed the religion (or lack of it) of their parents and grandparents. Sorting out a faith discipline today demands an honest look at ourselves. It's not just replacing old certainties with new ones. I don't have the luxury of taking my faith for granted. I want to find a way past the stereotypes of what a faith life is supposed to look like and get to the questions that really matter. That's a journey available to anyone willing to try, including—and perhaps especially—people like me who aren't supposed to take it seriously in the first place.

Notes

1. David Murrow, *Why Men Hate Going to Church* (Nashville: Nelson Books, 2005).

2. C. S. Lewis, foreword to Joy Davidson's *Smoke on the Mountain: An Interpretation of the Ten Commandments* (Philadelphia: Westminster Press, 1954) 7.

3. Barbara Brown Taylor, *Leaving Church: A Memoir of Faith* (San Francisco: HarperSanFrancisco, 2006).

4. From the Campus Crusade for Christ website, here are those laws: (1) "God loves you and offers a wonderful plan for your life"; (2) "All of us sin and our sin has separated us from God"; (3) "Jesus Christ is God's only provision for our sin . . ."; and (4) "We must individually receive Jesus Christ as Savior and Lord; then we can know and experience God's love and plan for our lives" (http://www.ccci.org/wij/index.aspx [accessed 11 December 2009]).

5. Wesley and the early Methodists' view was expressed in the words of one of Charles Wesley's hymns: " . . . unite the two so long divided, knowledge and vital piety, learning and holiness combined . . ."

CALLED TO SOMETHING

As Jesus passed along the Sea of Galilee, he saw Simon and his brother Andrew casting a net into the sea—for they were fishermen. And Jesus said to them, "Follow me and I will make you fish for people." And immediately they left their nets and followed him. As he went a little farther, he saw James son of Zebedee and his brother John, who were in their boat mending the nets. Immediately he called them; and they left their father Zebedee in the boat with the hired men, and followed him. (Mark 1:16-20)

Mark, in his Gospel, provides a short account of how Jesus called the first disciples. In our lives, we all hear and respond differently to that call, but to me this passage speaks of how God through Christ comes to us in our ordinary routines and leads us to see our lives in a different way. Beyond making new rules, he issues a call to life in all its fullness. About these disciples, Mark simply says, "for they were fishermen." I'm sure being a fisherman in those days took special skills: knowing how to live unencumbered, with patience, diligence, and faith. Life was tough, and I'm sure the disciples struggled to eke out a subsistence living and avoid the unpredictable hazards of the time. Jesus spoke to them in familiar words ("I will make you fish for something different"), challenging them to put their skills to work with a new purpose. He invited the disciples to take a new perspective on life—calling them away from simply making a living into making a life. Jesus calls us into life: "I came so that you may have life, and have it more abundantly" (John 10:10)—full measure, shaken together, running over.

A middle-class lifestyle protects many of us from obvious risks to our physical well-being, but other threats to our thoughts and spirits abound. I was always terrible at fishing—impatient and ready to move on if the fish didn't bite. The world beckons with a multi-channel universe, tantalizing us with images of possibilities always beyond our reach. What kind of exciting life do we think is going on somewhere else? Is there somewhere else we'd rather live, someone else we'd rather be with? Sooner or later, however, looking for the next new thing brings us up short.

What caused the disciples to drop everything that day and "immediately" follow Christ? He had a much greater vision for them than they could have for themselves. When left to our own devices, we collapse into narrow limits. For the early Jews, naming something meant they gained power over it. In his vision for Simon, Jesus gave him a new name, "Peter, the rock" (Matt 16:18). Peter was called to something better and given a name to fit. He was called out of himself in an irresistible way. This story reminds me that I need to provide a vision like that for my children. I need to let them know that I expect the future to hold great possibilities for them, that they are destined for something special. I don't want to pressure them, but to let them know that I see something great in them, something that may be difficult for them to imagine for themselves. A vision should be big enough to allow us room to grow into it; the grace of God calls us out of ourselves and into something infinitely bigger. That's why I'm not embarrassed to acknowledge that I am looking for something better in my life, something that lifts me out of myself, a bigger vision that I find in following Christ. The invisible God calls me to take a spiritual adventure within myself.

As a restless, modern, middle-class nomad, I want to be at home in my own soul and know that I belong wherever I am. That can be difficult. As an East Tennessean who feels most at home near the Great Smoky Mountains of my youth, I've never gotten used to the dry hills of central Texas. It's never truly felt like home to me. But one year leads to the next, and now my family and I have lived in Austin for more than twenty-five years. Initially, I didn't see myself as a typical suburban dweller, and for a long time I resisted buying a weed eater. I thought we would live here for a little while until something else came up. I figured we were just passing through. Now we've lived in the same house for more than two decades. Taking up this three-bedroom/two-bath lifestyle risks defining me in ways that don't always suit me. I always thought I would find a church like the one in which I grew up, that big cathedral-style Methodist church in downtown Knoxville. For me, that was church: stained-glass windows, huge pipe organ, professional-sounding choir, hard wooden pews, an ornate altar with a wooden sculpture of Gabriel holding his horn. (Gabriel was later demoted to the back of the church when someone decided Jesus should have the prime real estate in front.) I loved that church, and it was my template to evaluate any later candidates for a church home—meaning, of course, that the new ones always came up short. They were temporary stand-ins.

Going to church became less of a regular routine and began to depend on how motivated I felt from week to week. As with many young families, the arrival of kids motivated us to get more involved in a faith experience: celebrating Jewish holidays at home and attending church on Sundays. No place felt completely right, so we tried a church near our house for the sake of convenience until we found the ideal place. If the building were located just around the corner, maybe we might get there on time, or at least get there. When my family and I attended, I liked for us to sit in the back. I figured that was a good transitional move. (As I said, I'm not supposed to take church that seriously in the first place.) I was probably like some of the students in our bigger classes at the university who like to sit in the back row and read the campus newspaper. They show up out of routine, or because they don't want to be penalized for missing something. Now we've attended that "not-ideal" church for many years and been drawn deeply into its fellowship. I've come to accept this church community and allow myself to feel at home. The people I heard speaking about their stewardship, mission trips, and good deeds once seemed remote to me; but now I know them better, and I love them, and some of them love me too. Now I like to sit closer to the front.

At some point, I had to accept that "this is it," this is life, and dive in. I suppose I've grown to feel that way about other things too. While I've waited to find the perfect job, town, home, and church—endlessly distracting searches—my life has turned inward. That's where my biggest challenge lies. That's the kind of adventure I think the disciples responded to: to follow Christ, not to a bigger town, a bigger lake, a better synagogue, or a better job, which eventually always show their limits, but to an adventure within their own lives, which in God's hands is always unlimited.

We experience those inner lives partly through relationships. For people like me, the most challenging relationship lies in marriage. My call to discipleship reminds me that Paul's principle of "power in weakness" is true for husbands and wives. Working through the ups and downs of any long-term marriage reveals the paradox of how difficult it is to make ourselves vulnerable to those we are closest to and who seem to threaten us the least—but that's our best chance to experience real grace. Human relationships are often messy and don't always unfold according to the romantic ideal, but they invite us to the kind of true intimacy that the faith journey demands we take.

I was not much of a relationship person early in my romantic career and made no steady commitments. I'm sure I was looking for the perfect woman and not interested in anything less. In retrospect, I probably had "intimacy issues," and my initial encounter with my future wife was no exception. A few months after meeting and getting to know Carol, I went home for the holidays. That year, my mom died on New Year's Eve. Looking back, I can see how that powerful event helped pave the way for a deeper emotional connection. During that profound wounding experience, my grief opened a window through which I saw more of who I truly am. I became more available to someone else and open to deeper intimacy.

I have to keep relearning the principles of intimacy. Ego fights back, in spite of Paul's warning that love "does not insist on its own way" (1 Cor 13:4). Sometimes my kind of love does. I want things on my terms where I can control them. In marriage, as with any other relationship, I'm perfectly capable of wanting to manage the situation, to avoid uncomfortable issues, to selectively present the side of me that works to my advantage. I hold on to the little pieces of myself that I don't want to share, fearing I may somehow hem myself in. I'm sometimes afraid of what even seemingly innocent behaviors may signify if they were known, and I'm irritated at being obliged to account for myself. Professional men become adept at managing their image and the "situation," which isn't necessarily the kind of skill intimacy requires. That goes for supposed experts in issues of family and marriage. In his farewell sermon at the Episcopal seminary in Austin, Will Spong, professor of pastoral theology and noted counselor, reflected on his own divorce, saying, "I learned how much courage it took to tell the truth and how easy it is to be in this profession and lie about anything that makes you look bad."

In my family, we say "I love you" to each other on a regular basis, sometimes to the point of unconscious routine. Maybe it gets devalued with repetition, but it seems like a fitting way to close every phone call or leave-taking: "I love you" . . . "I love you, too." There are rare times when I may not feel like saying it, and even rarer times when I don't hear it back. As often as we've spoken them, though, I miss those words profoundly when I don't hear them. Life doesn't work as well when such an important part of it is damaged. It shames me when I do something to hurt my wife's feelings and makes me feel like a fraud in trying to say anything about the Christian life. It reminds me of how much emotional energy is wrapped up in a relationship.

Paul says many other things about love, including that it "rejoices in the truth." That doesn't mean love always likes what the truth is, but it has the power to rejoice in and through what those truths say. Fortunately, even the fear that I can't always love the way I want finds acceptance as an honest truth within my marriage. In the movie *Network*, based on Paddy Chayefsky's novel, the aging television news executive Max Schumacher ventures into a relationship with a hard-driving career woman from the same corporation but a different generation. He tries to draw her into a more satisfying intimacy by openly declaring, "This is not a script, Diana . . . I'm beginning to get scared . . . . You're dealing with a man that has primal doubts, Diana, and you've got to cope with it." When she asks, "What exactly is it you want me to do?" he replies, "I just want you to love me; I just want you to love me, primal doubts and all."[1] As Rabbi Julius Gordon has said, "Love is not blind—it sees more, not less. But because it sees more, it is willing to see less."

Our intimate relationships have an element of the holy that works like God's grace. My wife loves me in a way that overlooks whatever I do to earn it, and that enables me to love her back. I trust that I am still loved, even if I don't always act lovingly or feel loveable. The gospel lesson of God's grace gives me courage that I can love beyond my desire to put my own needs first. It's easy to regard the Christian life as a limit that keeps me from doing what I want rather than a liberating force. I know that a deeply intimate relationship like marriage can free me to be more of myself, not less. I want those closest to me to know who I really am and love me just the same. Intimacy grows with honesty, not through public relations and spin control. There is a great and often untapped capacity for grace and understanding between two people, and I've learned not to underestimate the capacity for love in my wife.

In the movie *About Schmidt*, Jack Nicholson plays a fairly typical new retiree. In the superficial platitudes at his company retirement dinner, he's conflicted about what it all means; this feeling intensifies when he leaves his old office after a visit, only to see the boxes of files containing his hard work set out for the trash. He conformed to the norms of society, worked reliably at his job, earned a living—and now he's not sure what it all meant. At home one day, he sees a charitable appeal on television and begins making regular contributions to support a young orphaned child in Africa. As the charity suggests, he begins writing to the little boy about himself and his life.

Much later, upon returning home to an empty house from his daughter's wedding, he reflects on the difference his life has made in the world—none that he can see. Relatively soon, he says, he will die (perhaps in twenty years, maybe the next day), and after that it will be as though he never existed.

Then he receives a letter in the mail from the six-year-old orphan. A nun wrote it for the boy, reporting that the child is bright and loves to draw. The boy enthusiastically looks forward to hearing Schmidt's letters read to him. He wishes Schmidt health and happiness, saying that he has sent a painting for him. Schmidt looks for the painting, opens and unfolds it, and gazes on a child's crayon sketch with stick-figure arms and legs—showing a man smiling and holding a little boy by the hand; the sun shines in a blue sky. Schmidt's eyes fill with tears. He stares at the image again and then, in the last moment of the film, through his tears he looks up with a smile of hope. Schmidt doesn't utter a word, but the scene speaks for itself. All the time he spent at work ultimately mattered far less than the gift of love he gave a little boy he had never met.[2]

I don't want to wait until the end of my life to learn Schmidt's lesson. Like the disciples, we are called to a journey outside the traditional measures of place and time so often used to mark our status and progress—outside the narrow limits of occupation and materialism. What have I learned? That there are other ways to explore a new life, and that I can be at home where I am. The most challenging frontiers lie within our hearts and within our relationships, and that's what draws me in. We're called to something better—to God's very best.

Notes

1. Network, dir. Sidney Lumet, Metro-Goldwyn-Mayer, 1977.

2. *About Schmidt*, dir. Alexander Payne, screenplay by Payne and Jim Taylor, New Line Cinema, 2002.

Chapter 4

A MAN'S MAN

When they stood him among the pillars, Samson said to the servant who held his hand, "Put me where I can feel the pillars that support the temple, so that I may lean against them." Now the temple was crowded with men and women; all the rulers of the Philistines were there, and on the roof were about three thousand men and women watching Samson perform. Then Samson prayed to the Lord, "O Sovereign Lord, remember me. O God, please strengthen me just once more . . . ." (Judges 16:25-28)

Many stories from the Scriptures have found their way into popular culture. You need not be religious to know a little about some of the major characters of the Judeo-Christian faith. I suspect much of the Bible resides in society's collective memory as a loose conglomeration of epic Cecil B. DeMille Technicolor film characters. Charlton Heston became the iconic Moses in *The Ten Commandments*,[1] and he played the title role of the chariot racer in *Ben-Hur*.[2] That character deserved to be in the Bible even if he wasn't. Hollywood's Heston merged completely with his film personas when he brought out a multi-media project giving himself top billing: *CHARLTON HESTON PRESENTS! the Bible.*

In another example of "cinematic Scriptures," the book of Judges tells the familiar story of Samson. It has all the necessary ingredients: a tragic, larger-than-life hero, sex, and violence. It seems like a simple tale of a man who fell for the wrong woman, Delilah. She's almost as famous as he is. Even a man of superhuman strength meets his downfall when seduced by a kryptonite temptress. We may picture Hedy Lamarr as Delilah and Victor Mature as the Hollywood Samson, with oiled up, rippling pects, wrestling a lion and fighting hundreds of Philistines with his bare hands. (Okay, he may also have used the jawbone of an ass, but it was still pretty impressive.) Of course, there is a deeper, more spiritual lesson than we might glean at first reading. For me to figure out what the story of Samson and others mean on a higher spiritual level, I need to come to terms with what the Bible means for me personally. For me, the book is a combination of Hollywood epic and iconic sacred charm, but it's also something much more deeply felt. Perhaps the Old Testament lends itself to the Hollywood treatment more often than the New, where many Christians find their personal attachment to the Bible compartmentalized in the Gospels. The films of Jesus seem to cause the most controversy, perhaps because they approach something that is too personal. But how do the parts of Scripture work together, and what am I to make of the combination? As I seek to understand my faith, I can't avoid confronting the Bible—an important vehicle of that faith, the channel through which it flows to me.

Growing up, I was exposed to the familiar passages, but reading the Bible was not a big part of my life or my worship practice. I absorbed many of the more common passages through choral music, seasonal religious events like Christmas pageants, and the larger culture. But actual Bible reading was more of a Baptist thing. Focusing on the Bible meant you were a "literalist" who considered every word inerrantly true from start to finish, Genesis to Revelation. That went a little too far for me. A preacher who emphasized Scripture excessively received the derogatory label of "Bible thumper." For the thumper, the Bible functioned like a theatrical prop. Rather than actually reading from it, he jabbed his finger at it from time to time, or lifted the book in the air for special emphasis. Still, I had the feeling he could quickly whip through those thin pages to find any passage that came to mind. The King James Version was preferred, of course. (After all, that's how God said it.)

For some, this emphasis on Scripture made the Bible something to read diligently, learning large chunks by heart. Some churches had memorization contests for kids. For others like me, I suspect it made the Bible more of a totem, not something anyone would actually pick up and read. The "family Bible" was a crucial fixture in many homes, like the household gods the ancient nomads carried around with them.[3] The totemic family Bible sometimes took on a special importance, especially to the extent that it recorded significant dates, births, deaths, weddings, and other personal genealogical notes. Somehow, my mother's clan lost track of my grandparents' Bible, and they searched for it relentlessly. To his frustration, some of them regularly asked my dad years after my mom had died if he was sure he hadn't seen it somewhere in her things. That Bible had an emblematic, mystical family importance far beyond its theological value.

We learned Scripture in Sunday school, of course, and I received a Bible when I joined the church at age nine—a traditional model with black cover, red edges, and my name in gold letters. I can still picture it grasped in one of the pastor's big hands and given to my small ones, and I never dared to write in it. Considering how little wear and tear I subjected it to, the book is still in great shape. In elementary school, I was taught basic Bible etiquette of the time: no other books were to be stacked on top of the Bible. I'm not sure where this rule originated; I don't think it's in the Bible. To be safe, though, I kept my copy on the shelf for a long time to avoid accidental desecration. For many of us "Southern Christians," the Old Testament, once you got past Adam and Eve, was not a big part of the scriptural landscape. We were taught to search the Gospels for the real message; the Old Testament (it was "old," after all) was simply a warm-up, and everything pointed to the coming of Christ. So somewhere between the Garden of Eden and Matthew, it all got a little hazy for me, kind of like those old maps for pre-Columbian sailors and their helpful warnings ("There be monsters here"). Legendary characters roamed that Scripture zone, probably crossing paths with Jason and the Argonauts and Hercules, although I think the dinosaurs were gone by that point. I read a lot of adventure stories back then, and I had a book of Old Testament Bible stories with color illustrations: the Tower of Babel, Moses parting the Red Sea, and Joshua destroying the walls of Jericho. I loved looking at them, just as I enjoyed the fanciful drawings for other tales, like "Ali Baba and the Forty Thieves." It was a vivid world back then for a young boy in pre-color/cable television days.

As my familiarity with Scriptures has grown, my approach to them has changed. The stories now resonate with me. They speak to me, or I suppose something speaks to me through them. They have become like old friends, and the maps of my knowledge—once rather hazy sketches—are colored in a little better. I've been able to take personal ownership of the sacred writings of my faith, wresting them from the Bible thumpers. I didn't like taking their word for it when they spouted "chapter and verse," but I lacked my own mastery. That's why I determined to plow through a 365-day version of the Bible (even writing in it) and made it through a couple of times, although it took me two or three years each time. It's not like hitting the highlights (there were a lot of "begats" to get through), but was a good way to make sure I didn't miss anything. Now at least I feel like nothing lurks there that has escaped me; I know where all the stories are hidden and can weave them into my theological imagination.

To reach that stage, though, I had to get past the inerrant literalism so "fundamental" to many Christians. Certainly, those perspectives were common where I grew up, as the radio evangelists (and probably many of the churches too) excoriated "liberal," pusillanimous, secular-humanist "so-called pastors" who dared to question the accuracy of God's word. The only church worthy of the name was a "Bible-believing" church. For years, a billboard in my hometown stood, appropriately, on top of the wonderfully smelling Kern's Bakery Company building: "Man does not live by bread alone . . . " (the sign excluded the corollary that followed: "but by every word that flows from the mouth of God," Matt 4:4). As a kid, not having learned to think poetically, I imagined how a diet of only bread could get a little old.

I suppose a literalist view makes religious life easier; starting from that first basic premise of inerrancy allows the Bible alone to dictate one's entire belief system. All questions can be referred to that bedrock principle. But I never do things the easy way. To start taking the Bible seriously in my life, I had to get past the association with anti-intellectualism. Modern scholarly analysis, such as the Jesus Seminars that began to strip away received wisdom about what the historical Jesus said and didn't say, posed a deep threat to some believers. For me, that analysis had the opposite effect. I have been guided by writers like John Shelby Spong, who in books including *This Hebrew Lord* and *Liberating the Gospels* has helped me see beyond my often troublesome questions about my religion.[4]

Here's my best personal understanding of how I approach the Bible. The "did this really happen?" kind of literalism—the kind I can't accept—locates Jesus inside history as a subject of objective, journalistic eyewitness accounts, and I don't believe that was the intention of the Gospel writers. Jesus preached and was interpreted after he was gone *within* synagogue worship, through "Jewish eyes." The early New Testament writers related this new spiritual figure and his message of love to familiar themes and stories in the available sacred texts. The Gospels were efforts to preach Jesus, to lift him out of specific historical circumstances and embed him in the universal structure of God's message revealed in Torah and the prophets. The "it all happened just like they said" literalism took hold only after the fracture between the early church and Judaism, an unfortunate schism that continues to this day, although there are increasing efforts to recuperate the enriching insights that are possible from one branch to the other. Understanding the Jewish roots of Jesus has certainly deepened my beliefs. Earlier in this book, I pose this question: How is it possible to take my faith seriously as a Christian married to a Jew? Maybe this explanation of my theological perspective helps explain it. I suppose it's possible for me in the same way it was for the early Christians. We're not so far apart.

Getting beyond inerrant literalism has made the Bible much more accessible to me in my spiritual life. Far from undermining my faith, the newer scholarly insights and more liberal interpretation of the Scriptures have freed the Bible to speak to me the way I believe God intends it to speak. I don't worry much about whether something actually happened, such as trying to figure out how a virgin birth was possible, or whether Jesus truly raised Lazarus from the dead and performed other nature-defying miracles. Christ himself is true, and the stories about him point to that greater truth. Something miraculous happened to the disciples. A better scholarly understanding of the Bible does not diminish the mystery of my faith or the invitation I feel to experience a message from God through Scripture.

As for Samson, what message does he have for me (Judg 16)? In addition to the Gospels, I find myself drawn to stories from the Old Testament. To my wife, I teasingly refer to them as "your guys," but they feel like my guys too. They speak to me easily now that I let them. As I reflect on the challenges facing men in particular, this story of a so-called "man's man" has a word for me. God didn't promise Samson's parents that he would give their son superhuman strength. The angel of the Lord said the boy would be a Nazirite from birth—no razor would come upon his head (as required by Mosaic Law for such cases). A Nazirite was a man set apart from the rest, consecrated to God by a special vow. God had a purpose for Samson and wanted to work through him to accomplish a plan. I've often wondered why Samson was foolish enough to tell Delilah about his hair. Hadn't she already demonstrated her capability of using his secret against him? Maybe he simply grew to take his strength for granted. He pushed the envelope. After she nagged him, Samson finally broke down and told Delilah that a razor had never touched his head. If his hair were cut, he would become like any other man. He said it, but I wonder if he actually believed it. He had always been able to get out of tight spots by using his strength. Why should this time be any different? Yes, his parents said he was special and chosen for a purpose. In addition to the key secret, Samson revealed to Delilah that he was consecrated to God. But that was a long time ago, before he was even born, and he had never tested the idea that his strength was from God. It was simply who he was.

When Samson revealed all to Delilah, he treated his special Nazirite status lightly, putting it at risk and squandering God's gifts. The Bible says that when his head was shaved, his strength left him, and when he woke up he did not know that the Lord had left him as well. God hadn't meant to make a simple bargain with Samson: you can be superman if you avoid cutting your hair. There was more to it. That's what makes it biblical. God wanted Samson's full attention, to work in his life, to bless him, to continue in covenant relationship with him his entire life. Samson was to be a Nazirite from the day of his birth to the day of his death. The hair was merely an outward symbol, visible evidence of a special vow. Now even the outward symbol was gone.

Didn't Samson do what many of us do? For what should be an inner spiritual commitment, we substitute our outer practices. Those include "hows" of belief such as the fundamentalizing of belief and Scripture. Nothing in the story suggests that Samson had much of a relationship with God. He assumed that his ritual observance was the whole point, that his strength lay in his hair. But that wasn't the point. God honored God's side of the commitment, blessing Samson with strength, but Samson didn't live up to his side of the bargain. Instead, he was strong headed and willful, wanting what he wanted when he wanted it. He saw a Philistine woman he wanted as a wife and told his dad to get her for him. The first time he speaks to God, he says, "I'm hungry. Give me some food." Samson had a gift, but he was undisciplined and unable to direct his gifts toward productive ends. Relying on his own strength, he lost sight of his true purpose, and that made him an easy target.

The only other time Samson speaks to God in the story is at the end, when he is captured and displayed for the Philistines. Finally, he is blinded and obliged to confront his own dependence and utter vulnerability. Only then does he enter into the kind of intimate relationship with God that God desired all along. The story stands on its own, but in looking backwards from a New Testament perspective, I see it foreshadowing my Christian theology: God's power made perfect in weakness. The Bible has a way of turning common sense upside down in this recurring paradox, as God works through the last, the youngest, and the weakest. As Paul said, "When I am weak, then I am strong" (2 Cor 12:10). Samson asked his attendant to help him find the giant pillars of the temple, and he reached out and felt them. After feeling the pillars, Samson at last called to the Lord in heartbreaking simple sincerity: "Lord God remember me . . . and strengthen me only this once" (Judg 16:28). He didn't ask God to make him a strong person, but rather to obtain strength for a special purpose. When he pulled down the temple, when his gifts and purpose were aligned in a relationship with God, the Bible says he was able to destroy many more of the enemy in that moment than he ever did in his lifetime.

In my life, God often needs to blind me to the things that distract and worry me. I need to reach out and feel the important tasks that need my attention, right then and there—not sometime in the distant future, not somewhere outside my reach. Even if those tasks seem as heavy as the giant pillars in Dagon's temple, I need to find them, touch them, and begin. I may need help locating them, but then I can ask for strength to accomplish the task at hand. God gives strength not only to make us strong, but to allow us to do something with that strength. How many times do we treat our special gifts lightly, substituting outer piety for a true inner and intimate relationship with God? For me, among the many messages that God speaks throughout the Scriptures, this one says I need to be blinded to everything except the pillars in my life that are right in front of me. Some blinding to the many distractions of life is often necessary in order to force me inside myself to something deeper. That's where God waits for me to ask to "remember me" and strengthen me for the purpose at hand.

Notes

1. Dir. Cecil B. DeMille, written by Ingraham et al., Motion Picture Associates, 1956.

2. Dir. William Wyler, screenplay by Karl Tunberg, Metro-Goldwyn-Mayer, 1959.

3. In Genesis 31, when Jacob escapes from his father-in-law Laban, Rachel steals her father's gods for good measure. Laban seems to want his gods, sheep, and daughters back in that order.

4. *This Hebrew Lord* (New York: Seabury Press, 1974); *Liberating the Gospels: Reading the Bible with Jewish Eyes* (San Francisco: HarperSanFrancisco, 1996).

Chapter 5

ABUNDANCE OF THE HEART

For out of the abundance of the heart the mouth speaks. (Matthew 12:34)

. . . do not worry about how you are to speak or what you are to say; for what you are to say will be given to you at that time; for it is not you who speak, but the Spirit of your Father speaking through you. (Matthew 10:19-20)

. . . for I have not spoken on my own, but the Father who sent me has himself given me a commandment about what to say and what to speak. (John 12:49)

Pray also for me, so that when I speak, a message may be given to me to make known with boldness the mystery of the gospel . . . . Pray that I may declare it boldly, as I must speak. (Ephesians 6:19-20)

For much of my childhood, I was conscious that I had a problem with speaking. I often stuttered, which led to embarrassing moments. In fourth grade, I asked my teacher to let me submit a report in writing rather than having to stand in front of the class and deliver it aloud. The following year, another teacher called on students to answer math problems. My tension mounted as my turn approached. I knew the answer was "30," but I couldn't get the word out: "Thhhhhirrrrrr . . . ." My classmates laughed, upsetting me deeply. Shortly, notes of apology started arriving at my desk. My friend, David, had passed the word that the others would have to answer to him if they didn't quickly tell me they were sorry. I appreciated his gesture, but I knew it was only a short-term solution. In the years that followed, I continued to fear public moments when I wouldn't be able to say what I wanted, when the words simply wouldn't come out. I wished I could say what was on my mind as casually and easily as my friends. From that experience, I realized how our ways of speaking are deeply personal, and I understood the luxury of being unhindered in saying what's on our minds.

I also learned the importance of teachers in the lives of young people. When I was a junior in high school, my drama teacher, Miss Long, pulled her chair next to me one day and said, "Let's talk about what part you are going to perform in the next play." *Uh oh*, I thought, *I'm not sure I like the direction this is going.* I already felt butterflies in my stomach, imagining freezing on stage, unable to get the lines out. The play was Arthur Miller's *The Crucible*, and Miss Long thought I should portray Thomas Putnam, a wealthy landowner fearful of witchcraft. I took her up on her invitation, and somehow it worked because she had a vision for what I could do. It was a pleasure to speak lines and hear them come out smoothly. My teacher's confidence in me inspired my confidence in myself.

As we get older, it may be tough for men to say what's on our minds, but for me at least it's now less a matter of stuttering—the causes of which are still unclear and partly genetic. One can't simply decide to "get over it." But, like so many things in life, once one becomes aware of a difficulty, it is easy to become absorbed with it until it grows out of proportion. It lurks in the background like an unwanted guest, ready to let itself in when we least want it. Through my minor role in *The Crucible*, I took a major step toward my fear, resulting in greater confidence and leading me to seek and even enjoy opportunities for public speaking. Later, I took on-air jobs in radio, and speaking to groups is a regular part of my work as a teacher. I was routinely confident in my early professional life and carefree about standing in front of a big class.

In recent years, however, the old "thorn" has taken on a new shape in my life. Paul used that term, saying he thought God gave him a thorn in the flesh to keep him from being too "elated" (2 Cor 12:7). Given the confidence I enjoyed for so many years, this development seems like a cruel irony. I thought I was beyond it. I don't stutter anymore, but sometimes I experience keen feelings of anxiety—in a car going over a high bridge, cramped in a tight window seat on a crowded plane, and sometimes before an important class or speech. In recent years, I notice it when I'm in a formal situation with a crowd, in a situational box of expectations that I can't escape. Public moments bring the most difficult manifestation of this anxiety, when it strikes directly at the heart of my personal and professional identity. This adult-onset "stage fright" is not so bad that it hinders my career (others apparently don't notice it), but is serious enough to get my attention. These moments of fear carry an important lesson for me: that rather than becoming absorbed in my own self and abilities, I need to become more focused outside myself, to depend moment to moment on God and know that God can use me even in (and particularly in) my weakness. That is a hard lesson.

I've noticed my new "thorn" in situations like college commencement. In spite of participating in them countless times, they began to cause me great anxiety. Being in an administrative role makes these events command performances. Given the size of our school, graduation events are always held in a gigantic university sports arena, the only venue spacious enough to hold all the graduates and their families. Once the graduates march in to take their places, the faculty lines up in a double row near the back entrance, waiting for the orchestra to strike up the processional music. I wear my dad's black doctoral-style robe, which he passed on to me when he retired, with the satin hood hanging down the back in the "Old Gold" colors of the University of Iowa. I have a black mortarboard hat that I prize because I finally found one large enough to fit on my head without falling off. Then we make our entrance accompanied by the usual pomp and circumstance and march into the cavernous hall, filing in with thousands of graduates and their parents turned around to see us make our dignified, pompous way to the stage and our assigned seats. There I have to sit for what seems like forever, but is actually closer to two hours, on the front row, highly exposed with nowhere to escape, under bright lights, and wearing a hot academic gown. I confess that it becomes unnerving as I sit with sweaty palms and dry mouth, light-headed, wishing to be anywhere else but there.

One year, my mind even played tricks on me, telling me I had heard my cue to head to the podium and announce names. When I realized my gaffe, I recovered and executed a diversionary move to a nearby seat. At moments like that, although I'm embarrassed to admit it, I even wondered whether I could continue in a career path that expected me to perform at such events. This was, after all, only the ceremony for my own college. What must it be like for the president to preside over full commencement exercises for the entire university, so large one year that they were held in the football stadium? I had new respect for the Pope and the Queen of England, whose jobs include many such events. The Pope can't excuse himself in the middle of mass simply because he starts feeling jumpy. This feeling doesn't fit the way I prefer to think about myself. It makes me feel foolish, and I don't like it. In fact, I hate it. I'm supposed to be confident and capable. I'm sure no one noticed anything amiss, but most of life's struggles take place out of public view. Like other things that challenge me, I've tried to understand what this anxiety means within the context of my spiritual life. What message or lesson does God have for me? How will I cope with this thorn when it pricks me?

I remember a particular day in May before the big spring commencement event one year. As the day grew closer, I began to get apprehensive. I prayed hard about it and even went to my church sanctuary on the morning of the ceremony to help me relax, and if the pastors had been there I would have asked them to pray with me. This couldn't wait until Sunday. Of course, I read the usual passages from the Bible that urge us "don't be anxious," "don't worry"—easier said than done. I thought about Moses, who because of his difficulty in speaking much preferred that God choose Aaron for the out-front role. But God found a way to use Moses and many other unlikely candidates. I have to believe God will use me too—in spite of, and even by way of my self-perceived limitations and apprehensions. Times like this drive me to seek God persistently and urgently. God doesn't want us to be anxious or fearful but to believe that God's grace is sufficient.

The amateur psychologist in me realizes that my anxious moments often come about because of my excessive focus on myself, my morbid overemphasis on the state of my emotions. The more I think about dreading the moment, the more I dread it. Just like when I was a kid and dreaded stuttering, my anticipation of the problem becomes a self-fulfilling prophecy. The moment I can get outside myself and find a way to lift my circumstances up to God, I can begin to accept this particular thorn. On the commencement stage that day in May, I confess that God was never far from my mind, which I suppose is a mindfulness I should seek all the time. I thought about the many ways I am blessed. I imagined my parents and grandparents, and what the writer of Hebrews calls the "unseen cloud of witnesses," watching me proudly from the back of the arena—those who had done so much to enable me to be in that place. I asked God to bless each one of the graduates and their families and to grant them success in their careers. In the case of one graduate, I knew her mother had died a few days before the ceremony, and she would say a few words to dedicate her achievement to her mother. I passed her a note of encouragement beforehand, saying that she would be in my prayers during the ceremony. I needed to get outside myself. This was a milestone event for our students and their families, a celebration of what we do as teachers. I prayed that whatever small role I played in the ceremony would be a part of that blessing.

As much as we are urged to "be not afraid," it's tough to obey. That's because to be unafraid, I am called to surrender my narrow frame of reference and allow myself to be absorbed into something bigger than myself: "Fear not, and be not dismayed at this great multitude; for the battle is not yours but God's . . . . You will not need to fight in this battle; take your position, stand still, and see the victory of the Lord on your behalf" (2 Chr 20:15-17). With a spiritual perspective, I should strive to be there, to be me, to be used—to take my position and watch what God accomplishes through me.

As department chairman, one of my duties in the ceremony was to read the names of my program's hundred or more graduates as they came to the stage to receive their diplomas. They turn in cards in advance to show us how they want their names pronounced, and I looked those over carefully to make sure I didn't mangle them too badly during their big moment. After the introductions and obligatory future-looking speech by an invited dignitary, the commencement marshals organized the seniors into a long line to approach the stage, hear their names announced, and receive their diplomas. Though urged not to, friends and family members inevitably shout frantically, blow airhorns, and applaud their graduates. The students get their diplomas, shake hands with the dean, and do something creative, silly, or celebratory for the crowd before returning to their seats. One film major shot his entire stage walk with a camera held at arm's length.

Shortly after I began reading the names and the first few graduates filed past my podium, I noticed a delay in the procession. To my left I saw a woman in a wheelchair being pushed up the ramp. Given the speedy efficiency of the first part of the ceremony and the many names yet to be called, I sensed the crowd getting restless with the break in the rhythm and the extra time. Furthermore, I realized that she intended to use a walker, being brought up behind her, to cross the stage and receive her diploma. As her assistant helped her out of the chair, I came around the podium to help hold the walker steady as she struggled to grasp the handles. Her mortarboard, shaken off in the effort, was carefully reattached, and then she was off under her own power across the stage to get her diploma.

After what seemed like an eternity in silence, the thousands of graduates, parents, faculty, and guests began to applaud, and then to stand, giving this determined woman a long and enthusiastic ovation. Watching her make her way to the other side of the stage brought tears to my eyes, and I was moved to praise God for her courage. This woman inspired me, lifted me beyond the routine of yet another commencement, and took me out of myself, just as I had asked. I gave thanks for being present at such a moment of courage and strength. I can't say I achieved perfect serenity during that particular commencement ceremony or ones that followed, but I have felt God's presence. As the Lord said to Paul, who asked three times for God to remove his thorn, "My grace is sufficient for you, for my power is made perfect in weakness" (2 Cor 12:9). Seeing the student in her wheelchair brought that message home to me again. If I can think of myself as an instrument, wishing to be used, to make my gifts available to bless others, then I can begin to relax in those moments. I can place the responsibility in stronger hands than mine. The disciples and Paul himself were not professional speakers and often must have worried about what they would say and how they would come across to their listeners. They were more effective witnesses when they had faith that God would speak through them. In Matthew's Gospel, Jesus says, "For out of the abundance of the heart the mouth speaks" (12:34). Our words inevitably reflect what's inside. When I performed in my high school play, I spoke lines that were written for me. Since then, I've wanted to share other messages, including the ones in this book. Like the disciples, I can be confident and bold to the extent that I have confidence in my message. Like Paul, I desire to speak boldly and with confidence out of an abundant heart. That lets me overcome whatever thorn jabs at me, for I speak not on my own behalf, but on behalf of the One who created me and gives me the words to speak.

Chapter 6

SPIRITUAL DRAMA OF EVERYDAY LIFE

These instructions are not mere words—they are your life. (Deuteronomy 32:47)

The stories of personal faith that seem to shout most loudly involve one overcoming some incredible challenge and enjoying the restoration of a broken life. The more dramatic the crisis, the more powerful the testimonial; these are supposedly God's "extreme makeover" success stories. I think, however, that the more difficult faith challenge for most of us—and for me—is nebulous and ongoing: not a specific conversion experience or crisis moment but the daily process of seeking an intentional relationship with God. This kind of success story may not pack the same drama, but it's one I wish I could live each day.

The conventional life crisis comes with loss, whether in work, family, relationships, or health. When that sort of loss accumulates, we picture it wrenching away the idea of a "normal" existence and leaving behind a screwed-up life. The success-story "heroes" overcome the gap between where they started and where they fell, clawing their way back to normal life. They "get their life back." But other kinds of gaps bring challenges just as great. Don't we all have nagging doubt about whether we can ever be the people we want to be? Even for those with a so-called regular life, the chasm is great between where we wish we could be and where we fear we may wind up. By most standards, my life has its share of success, but I know that, no matter how well I do, the threat of mediocrity or ordinariness lies just around the corner. I don't have to fail at my job to fall short of my ambition.

No matter how "normal" someone looks to me on the outside or how normal I look to others, I know that, as Thoreau said, most people "lead lives of quiet desperation."[1] Men especially are culturally conditioned to be quiet about it, to take care of business, even as ambition bumps against the reality of everyday life. Men like to hold God back until he's really needed: God as Plan B. We don't stop for directions; we keep going down the road. We don't play the God card unless the crisis demands it. It seems more natural to reach out for God when a noisy failure has our complete attention. But that's not a good spiritual strategy. How does one involve God in this kind of quiet and private failure, the ongoing everyday crisis to which we're all subject?

Why is it so difficult to find the path of faith that we long for and to adopt it as a daily discipline? Daily living is the invisible frontier of faith. It passes routinely as we are pressured by demands on our time, expectations of others, and habits that take us out of a mindful, waking discipleship. By definition, everyday life lacks the drama that may grab our attention, so its spiritual potential passes us by. But it's in our daily routines that we are called to step through that frontier into a more intimate walk with God. Mosaic Law emphasized the importance of daily observances, making faith instinctual and natural: "These commandments that I give you today are to be upon your hearts. Impress them on your children. Talk about them when you sit at home and when you walk along the road, when you lie down and when you get up. Tie them as symbols on your hands and bind them on your foreheads" (Deut 6:6-8).

Luke's Gospel picks up this idea when Jesus says, "If anyone would come after me, he must deny himself and take up his cross *daily* and follow me" (Luke 9:23, my emphasis). Intellectually, I know that a spiritual life should not be compartmentalized. Daily practices of prayer, reading, and reflection, when I can pull them off, give me a more seamless experience of God's presence. Writing reflections like these over the years has become like a faith journal to me, obliging me to put my experiences into words and making me more mindful of God's hand at work. Life is made of moments when I invite God to be a part of whatever situation is at hand, but it's easy to let the other routines of life crowd in. When the alarm goes off in the morning, we scramble to get kids to school and figure out the family schedule. Once at work, e-mails, voicemails, and knocks on the door compete for my attention, and before I know it another day is gone.

In contemporary culture, the endless appetite for new ways to manage busy lives has spawned an endless array of offers to help. Personal career coaches help us analyze, organize, and prioritize. I know I'm always looking for the right system to be more efficient at work, to get more done—preferably one that doesn't take a lot of effort. In an article in the *New York Times*, time-management expert David Allen said that working on these skills may take time but will lead to a greater sense of control and creativity. "Once you're freed from a feeling of overwhelm," he said, "you'll be freed up to focus on whatever it is that gives you inspiration in life."[2] Isn't this backwards? We are called first to seek God's presence in our lives, to seek God's will. Before I try to be more productive, I need to feel good about what I produce. Paul says, "But the fruit of the Spirit is love, joy, peace, patience, kindness, goodness, faithfulness, gentleness, and self-control. Against such things there is no law" (Gal 5:21-23). This idea of being "fruitful" reminds us to focus first on spiritual productivity.

The Bible contains several models of how to be fruitful, including ordinary people routinely asking God to bless their work and giving thanks for a successful result. David had that kind of daily discipline. In the Psalms he regularly confesses his moments of crisis, of quiet desperation, to God. In a way, he was saying, "God, things aren't going well, but I'm going to trust you, to remember once again and rejoice in those ways you've moved in my life before. You were with me then, and you're with me now."

The most important thing I can ask of God daily is to give me the confidence that God causes all things to work together for good in my life (see Rom 8:28). That sounds easy enough, but it's not. Here's where we get back to the fact that guys like to be in charge. We like to explain to God what we want, spell out our request list. However, being in relationship with God means surrendering authority, seeking direction, making ourselves available to God to use us for God's purpose. Most are conditioned to take on authority, to seek greater responsibility, to develop capable self-images. It feels contradictory to give up authority, to give up trying to be wise in our own sight. We may expect God to deal with us in our importance, helping us maintain what we have and adding more to it. This problem is illustrated in the Old Testament story of a military man and his search for healing. In 2 Kings, we learn of Naaman, who "was a great man in the sight of his master and highly regarded, because through him the Lord had given victory to Aram. He was a valiant soldier, but he had leprosy." Then Naaman heard about the prophet Elisha in Samaria, whom he hoped would cure him.

So Naaman went with his horses and chariots and stopped at the door of Elisha's house. Elisha sent a messenger to say to him, "Go, wash yourself seven times in the Jordan, and your flesh will be restored and you will be cleansed." But Naaman went away angry and said, "I thought that he would surely come out to me and stand and call on the name of the Lord his God, wave his hand over the spot and cure me of my leprosy. Are not Abana and Pharpar, the rivers of Damascus, better than any of the waters of Israel? Couldn't I wash in them and be cleansed?" So he turned and went off in a rage. Naaman's servants went to him and said, "My father, if the prophet had told you to do some great thing, would you not have done it? How much more, then, when he tells you, 'Wash and be cleansed'!" So he went down and dipped himself in the Jordan seven times, as the man of God had told him, and his flesh was restored and became clean like that of a young boy. (2 Kgs 5:9-14)

The case of Naaman shows how pride can blind us to God's work in our lives. Moreover, as we grow older and gain professional status, it gets more difficult to step out of the images, public and private, that we have spent so much time cultivating. Naaman was prideful, accustomed to pomp, obedience, and status. When Elisha told him to do a little thing, to jump in the river, he was insulted. He wanted something dramatic, something more in keeping with his expectations. A valiant soldier, a victorious military leader, Naaman had every reason to take pride in his accomplishments. In spite of all his worldly success, he badly needed healing, and so he sought someone he hoped could do it. He charged up to Elisha's house with horses and chariots and a large entourage, ready for Elisha to leap into action. But Elisha didn't even come out, enraging Naaman and wounding his image. Fortunately, his wise counsel urged him to swallow his pride and be obedient—open to the idea that God often asks us for something simple. Expecting something spiritually dramatic from God leads us away from the steady discipline of doing the daily small things that lead to a deeper faith.

Most days I'm involved in my job as a college teacher, and so inevitably much of my daily faith discipline gets played out in that realm. One might think academics should be good at spiritual discipline. We know the value of investing time in study and taking time to reflect, so surely we have the ability to think abstractly about something as challenging as the "invisible God." Somehow, though, my career doesn't seem to make my spiritual life any easier. My challenge is to see my job through the lens of my faith, to focus on being fruitful on a daily basis, with the confidence that other levels of productivity will follow naturally. The book of James gives a special admonishment for would-be teachers: "Not many of you should become teachers, my brothers and sisters, for you know that we who teach will be judged with greater strictness" (3:1).

James would not prevent people from becoming teachers; he simply wanted to emphasize the importance of a teacher's responsibility. Teachers don't merely pass along information; they help shape others' lives. James anticipates one of the pitfalls of the occupation, the possibility that we begin to act out of our own ego and pride rather than a genuine desire to serve students with sensitivity toward their own needs and difficulties.

The advice of James reminds me of a friend and colleague I knew for more than twenty years: James Tankard. I remembered getting to know Jim when he was a senior faculty member after I first arrived at the university. Sizing up my new colleagues, I wondered in his case how such a quiet and unassuming fellow could teach effectively. I had the arrogance of a newly minted Ph.D., approaching the job of teaching—especially graduate students—as a struggle: it was me against them to see who was smarter. If I was caught short in my understanding or knowledge, I considered it a defeat. I didn't see how Jim, a Stanford Ph.D. notwithstanding, could hold his own in that kind of combat. To satisfy my curiosity, I eavesdropped once outside the door of Jim's seminar and actually had a hard time hearing much of anything. He said a few quiet words, but I could tell he had the students' complete attention. In time, I understood that Jim modeled Paul's principle of "power made perfect in weakness." By not imposing his ego and attempting to dominate a class and show his knowledge, he allowed students to become more fully themselves. Many years later, Jim developed lung cancer, which made his voice even more difficult to hear as the illness progressed. It didn't matter, though: his students still hung on every word.

Not long after he retired, I learned from his wife that Jim didn't have much longer to live, so I paid him a last visit. I sat next to him on the couch so I could hear him better. His body had shrunk, but his spirit was still strong. I shared a saying with him from one of our Korean colleagues: "The best way to honor our teachers is to exceed them." Jim said he thought the Koreans were on to something. Teaching is a job that is not accomplished by force. The best teachers draw their students out of themselves, helping them become better. Such teachers step aside and let something special happen. When a teacher does that, students never regard it as weakness. Instead, it is a special kind of power.

Every teacher finds a unique way to operate, one that's closely bound up in the individual's personality. Teaching is naturally closely tied to one's self-image. If a class goes well or students tell me they enjoyed something I said, it lifts me up; when even a single comment is critical, it discourages me. That criticism can get personal. Every registration period on our campus, students used to set up what they call the "slam tables" near the center of campus. Sheets of paper are taped to the tables and labeled by course for passersby to scribble comments—some favorable but many vicious—about what they thought of a class and its instructor. As the days go by, the anonymous reviews fill the sheets and the tables, often competing for the most scathing comment. Of course, I can't resist checking them out, but it's best done when I'm in a good mood in case I'm in store for a negative zinger. Some may even start out positive but take a nasty turn. In one of the milder exchanges, one began, "Steve is a real intellectual," but it later expanded with "No, he's just a pseudo-intellectual." Ouch.

When I first began my career, I was a more confident teacher in some ways than I am now. I didn't know enough to know what I didn't know. Time is a great humbler. Even after all these years, I often have classic pre-semester dreams: the class has started and I don't know where to find the classroom or my notes. I'm woefully unprepared. Sometimes I picture the upcoming group being the same one I had the term before, and I will have to take them to an even higher level, but I can't because I've already taught them all I know. What if they discover I've run out of knowledge? Fortunately, though, I remind myself that I will encounter new students. They haven't heard what I have to say. (I might even be able to recycle some of my jokes.) Sometimes I don't feel like I have a lot to say. But on those days, I try to rethink my attitude. Of course, I have something I want to say and a structure in which to say it, but I am also there in part simply to spend time with students, to make myself available to them for whatever develops during the class. Although this is more easily done in smaller groups, teaching is an opportunity for me to be in a spirit of relationship with my students. I am sure I don't have all the answers, but we can work together to understand what we want to know. If teaching is only transmitting information, then once I do that my value is used up. But if I approach it as a more collegial process, then I build a relationship with value that continues on.

I rediscovered this truth a few years ago in an introductory seminar for doctoral students, designed to introduce them to the field and an academic career. I was overcommitted and worn out, and on occasion I felt unprepared to meet with them for the three-hour period, wondering if I truly had anything to tell them that they didn't already know. When that feeling struck, I reminded myself that the main thing I had to offer was myself, my time, and my willingness to help them understand their possibilities while being transparent about my personal challenges. I found myself becoming more personal than before, sharing experiences from my career that I hope were more self-reflective than that staple of the unprepared teacher: the proverbial "war stories." Becoming vulnerable comes more easily for me now with some success already behind me. We spent a lot of time talking about the meaning of "productivity" and easing the concerns many of them had about their professional futures. When it was time for the students to "grade" the professor on the end-of-semester instructor comments, I received the highest evaluations of my career from that class. I had given more of myself.

I still confront the challenge of rising expectations—my own and the ones I suspect others have of me. Of course, I see some of myself in Naaman. I'm certainly capable of acting out of the pride of position and senior status. I easily slip into letting ego guide my actions, thinking I need to be more and do more to justify my reputation. The public aspect of academic work makes it easy to compare ourselves to others. Our professional resumes go with us from job to job, and we post them on our websites for anyone to see. How do I measure up? No matter how much professional recognition I receive, it is never enough. There's always more I could do. Of course, that kind of drive helps a person succeed in such a relatively autonomous job. While we have accountability, professors also enjoy a tremendous amount of freedom, as my friends in the business world (what they like to call the "real world") are fond of reminding me. The new junior professor is hired and told in effect, "Here's your office, your phone, and your computer; we'll be back in five years to see if you have a national reputation!"

On one hand, it would seem that advancing toward more professional recognition would lead to greater confidence, security, and ease, but it can also result in dysfunction. It's easy to blame students, colleagues, and the administration for one's shortcomings, to be easily offended at slights to one's reputation, to spend too much energy in gamesmanship and self-promotion. Although these issues play out in other professions, the open-ended nature of academic work seems to make them particularly acute. The stakes get higher.

Avoiding these pitfalls requires that I avoid becoming too wrapped up in my status. Pride based on superior knowledge is tenuous and difficult to sustain because the field changes constantly, and the amount of knowledge continues to grow exponentially. I hope instead for an identity based on servanthood, my ability to discover and bring out important qualities in my students, to model an approach to learning and life that encourages their best. The focus must not be on my ego but on others. "Lord, let me be fruit-ful." With that attitude in the forefront of my thinking, I can get on with the business of being productive and not worry about whether it will be enough (because, of course, it can never be "enough"). When I look ahead at a coming year, I can easily despair of getting everything done. But looking back on a full year, I can see the amount of work I did and the wealth of experiences that came my way.

Not long ago, for the first time in several years, I had a large lecture class of 300 students. I wondered if I could still do a good job, if I could hold their attention. Students are easily bored, and attention spans are short. If given enough time to brood about it, I became downright daunted by the prospect. I wondered how I was able to do it so cavalierly when I first started out at age twenty-eight. Whatever qualms I may have over a small seminar are magnified in the mega-class. The large-lecture format takes a certain amount of self-confidence, even swagger, to pull off, but that still means I want all 300 students to love me, to hang on every word. Somewhere inside, it bothers me when inevitably they don't. But they won't all love me, and there's no way I can make them. I know I'd set myself up for disappointment if that were my standard for success. I have to admit that, on many mornings before class, I spent time in quiet reflection, praying that God would give me new insight and understanding, sharpen my mind, help me use my gifts to provide a valuable experience for my students, bless our time together, and allow me to do my best. In the servant role, my confidence was more secure, because that is a sincere motivation little related to ego. The answered prayer was that I felt like I grew during that time and had fun teaching the class, and from my conversations with students, it seems that they had fun too.

As a teacher, I'm still learning, especially about the importance of put-ting my discipleship into daily practice, of approaching my work with the right priorities. In the story of Naaman, his health crisis finally made him ready to play the God option, to have God "fix" him dramatically—accord-ing to *Naaman's* script. In the Gospel of Matthew, another military man makes a better model for me. He also sought healing—but it was a deeper healing for someone other than himself.

> When Jesus had entered Capernaum, a centurion came to him, asking for help. "Lord," he said, "my servant lies at home paralyzed and in terrible suffer-ing." Jesus said to him, "I will go and heal him." The centurion replied, "Lord, I do not deserve to have you come under my roof. But just say the word, and my servant will be healed. For I myself am a man under authority, with soldiers

under me. I tell this one, 'Go,' and he goes; and that one, 'Come,' and he comes. I say to my servant, 'Do this,' and he does it." When Jesus heard this, he was astonished and said to those following him, "I tell you the truth, I have not found anyone in Israel with such great faith . . . ." Then Jesus said to the centurion, "Go! It will be done just as you believed it would." And his servant was healed at that very hour. (Matt 8:5-10, 13)

The Roman centurion didn't demand a dramatic action on the part of Jesus; instead, he had confidence in a dramatic outcome. Jesus merely needed to say the word, the right word sought in faith, to produce a great result. The centurion had a powerful belief that a moment's brief encounter with Christ was enough. In the New Living Translation, Jesus says, "What you have believed has happened." This soldier led a hundred men, but his occupation had not led him to *command* that Jesus heal his servant or *demand* that he be treated with the status of his rank. I think Jesus was so impressed with the centurion because he was able to subordinate his professional image to his deeper, more authentic spiritual identity. With humility and a spirit of expectation and trust, he asked that Jesus simply speak a word of healing.

I'll try to remember to be more like the centurion and less like Naaman, to seek a simple word of healing in Christ, to not risk missing out on a blessing while I wait for God to do something dramatic. The drive for professional success, the everyday crisis of quiet desperation and unfulfilled ambition, can hinder spiritual productivity. God is doing dramatic things in my life all the time. He's waiting to do more, if I'll just ask him and daily put myself "under authority."

Notes

1. Henry David Thoreau, *Walden*, 1854, ch. 1

2. Cheryl Dahle, "Resolving to Break Time-wasting Habits," *New York Times*, 9 January 2005, http://query.nytimes.com/gst/fullpage.html?res=9907EED81139F93AA35752C0A 9639C8B63.

Chapter 7

STRUGGLE FOR SUCCESS

And Jacob said, "O God of my father Abraham and God of my father Isaac . . . . I am not worthy of the least of all the steadfast love and all the faithfulness that you have shown to your servant, for with only my staff I crossed this Jordan; and now I have two companies." (Genesis 32:9-10)

In my professional life, it's natural to be goal-directed, always looking to the future. Where is my "career path" going? Am I on schedule? How am I doing compared to my peers? What will I be able to accomplish during the time allotted for my career? Have I been and will I be a success? Professional success means producing, achieving, and advancing—getting and having. I didn't think much about that kind of index after college, but by graduate school I realized I had found something I was good at. Somewhat to my surprise, I seemed better at it than many others who tried it. That's a good thing, because after bouncing around a few majors during my undergraduate years and a few part-time jobs afterward, I wasn't sure I would find a career to be passionate about. Finding the academic path was like coming upon a crowd of people heading down the street. It looked like an interesting group. "Where's everybody going? . . . That sounds good, I think I'll join you for a while." A few blocks later, I found myself closer to the front. "What happened to those other guys?" They got tired or quit. I didn't think I was going that fast, but I liked it near the front. Then the comparisons kicked in as I felt compelled to measure myself against others with my now more lofty aspirations. Now, from the perspective of mid-career, I've thought a lot about my work and find myself using it as a lens on my spiritual life, trying not to compartmentalize one from the other. Both realms are closely tied to questions of personal identity and self-worth: Do I matter? Am I making a difference?

A career doesn't take a continuous upward path of progress. When we're younger, the possibilities of job and lifestyle seem unlimited, but as time goes by we confront a progressively more limited path produced by our life choices. The 401(k) retirement plan, which seemed like such a remote and abstract concept when I first started my job, has become much more relevant—tantalizing me to go online periodically to check its ups and downs. Contemplating even the idea of retirement reminds me that not all of my dreams—career and otherwise—will come true, and confronting that reality brings disillusionment. We all face that moment of truth when we reconcile our hopes with reality, coming to terms with what success really looks like.

Quiet failures accumulate over time, creating—acutely in the case of men—an inevitable gap between ambition and reality that leads to the well-known "mid-life crisis." As Richard Rohr describes it in his writings on the spiritual lives of men and women, the heroic ascending journey of the young man culminates in middle life in a "crisis of limitation," when he bumps up against the limits of his possibilities. To navigate that period successfully and continue on a "wisdom journey," the crisis must be transformed through a "descent." That "letting go," which Rohr says is the basis for all great spirituality, requires humility and honesty, qualities that professional men in particular often find difficult to master. Alternatively, Rohr says, many men react to the crisis by trying to maintain their "ascent," unable to find their real identity outside of their work and their toys, leading eventually to their becoming what he calls the archetype of the embittered "old fool."[1] One of the more extreme examples is the sad case of J. Howard Marshall II, the Texas oil billionaire and former Yale Law School professor who met Anna Nicole Smith when she was a twenty-something stripper and married her when he was eighty-nine. In his struggle to avoid his own descent, his wealth and intelligence didn't stop him from becoming a pathetic tabloid news character, entangling his great wealth among his heirs after his death, continuing long after the death of Anna Nicole herself. Not many of us have Marshall's kind of money, but the affluence of American culture makes it easier than ever to postpone, perhaps indefinitely, the moment of reckoning by losing ourselves in the distractions of materialism and upward mobility.

Rabbi Harold Kushner, in *Living a Life that Matters*, wrote of his own striving to meet two basic human needs: to feel successful and important, and to think of himself as a good person, someone who deserved the approval of others. He found in Genesis a model for this struggle in the life of Jacob, who fascinates us because he is a person who grows from an unlikable trickster who cheated his brother Esau out of his birthright to a mature man of faith. In a crucial event in Jacob's life, he wrestled in the desert one night with a mysterious figure who renamed him Israel (one who struggles with God). In Kushner's interpretation, Jacob struggled with his own conscience: his desire to be successful, to get what was coming to him no matter what, in conflict with his growing need to think of himself as a good person. He emerged from his wrestling match with a new integrity.[2]

Being successful in the professional world doesn't prevent us from seeking spiritual integrity. But we can easily get wrapped up in the routines of work and distracted by the quest for upward mobility. The questions of what it all means are put off, if we ever get around to them at all. It's easy to get our identity—professional and spiritual—handed to us instead of generating it ourselves. I guess that's where the hard work of faith comes in, when we start doing the work on ourselves that no one else can do for us. When I think about my menial jobs as a high school kid and in college, I'm incredibly grateful for the job I enjoy now, which gives me a great deal of personal autonomy. I always hated being told what to do. But that means I have to make decisions for myself—in my work and my faith life.

A few years ago, I received a gift of uninterrupted time and freedom to read and think, something I had desired for twenty years. That gave me plenty of time to reflect on these issues of success. During that time, I was free of the bureaucratic duties of my job and the regular class schedule. I stepped down as director of a school at the university and received time off from regular teaching to transition back into my faculty role. In the academic world, a sabbatical leave sometimes is granted every seven years for a semester or so to allow for rejuvenation and deep reflection—the same idea behind taking time off every seventh day for Sabbath rest. A sabbatical is not common in the business world, and it's not a tradition at my university, so I felt grateful for the opportunity. Even so, I found it strangely disorienting.

A sabbatical is challenging for the same reason we find it hard to honor the Sabbath. To stop working for a day, to honor the Sabbath as a spiritual principle, means having faith that the necessary work will still get done, but also that work isn't everything, that we are more than our work. We are not to idolize our work. Taking time off contradicts our business-oriented culture, which values productivity and tells us we will fall behind schedule and get off track. Of course, staying busy and preoccupied can be a psychological screen and a crutch. How many workers live in slavery to their routines, reluctant to take time off for fear of what may happen? They take pride in working long hours, coming in early and on weekends, and never taking a vacation. Time spent working has become the familiar measure of professional worth. The open-ended nature of many professional jobs, combined with the ever-present laptops and cell phones, means we can work all the time, wherever and whenever we want. Men, particularly, too often let their occupations define them. Put any two of us together for the first time, and the conversation quickly turns to what we do in our work as a way to describe ourselves, and where we fit in the social hierarchy. Of course, we would all like to feel that we are employed toward a useful purpose, that we produce something of value. Given that work is where we spend most of our time, we have to believe it amounts to something. The Apostle Paul himself was a tentmaker and advocated that others have a trade. However, it's often easy to use the way society values work to tell ourselves how well we're doing: hours spent at the office, salary, and the "stuff" that salary provides.

During the first few weeks of my time away, I had to detach myself from situations at work that I was accustomed to worrying about. That took a while. Of course, part of me wished my colleagues would have a tough time surviving without me, that no one would be able to do the job as well as I did. But institutions find a way to grind forward. Letting go meant understanding my new role and identity without the routines and trappings—modest though they were—of my previous job that had become part of my self-image. I used to be at the center of things, part of the rhythm of the place, and now I wasn't. I used to know what was going on, and now I didn't. Certainly, the family routine went on as before, and I continued with those responsibilities. It's strange how being at home all day made the evenings feel different. I was accustomed to coming home from work and plopping down in front of the TV in my La-Z-Boy, but now I could do that any time during the day. Knowing that took the fun out of it. I didn't have anything from which I could legitimately "rest." I missed the alternation between traditionally defined labor and relaxation. I still did mental labor, reading a big stack of books, writing notes, staring out the window and thinking, but it didn't feel the same. Labor is when you go into an office and "do" something: have a meeting, open mail, make a few calls, break for lunch. Even teaching class is helpful in making a day feel productive because it's a specific appointment with real time spent and real people engaged. Something happens; it's on the schedule.

That's why when people ask me about my job, they usually zero in on what classes I teach and how often. My ideas are much less tangible, and ideas were the focus of this time away from work. Thinking is exhausting in other ways, and it takes time, often without much to show for it. My older son was a high school senior at the time and the last to leave the house in the mornings to drive himself to school. As he went out the front door, he said good-bye to me, usually while I sat on the couch reading, still not dressed or showered. He told me later, with a laugh, that that was when he decided he wanted to be an academic himself one day. But this is not easy! Sometimes I think it would be nice to have a manual-labor job—drive a truck, build a wall, go home at the end of the day, and forget about it. "What did you do today, Steve?" "I built that wall over there." But then I remember that I don't like people telling me what to do.

Two routines on which feelings of success are often based were missing in my life. I wasn't putting in hours at an office, and I wasn't producing tangible products (yet): whether books, articles, or the teaching of students. How was I "productive"? Who was I now?

Every occupation has a yardstick that tells its members whether they measure up. As an academic, our ideas are our stock in trade. Having good ones and writing about them means you "matter." It's "publish or perish." It's a nebulous and tantalizing feeling that some special insight or discovery will add to the pool of knowledge. In my fantasy life, I dream that I will write a famous book, reviewed in the *New York Times* and called "a magisterial work." The president's advisors will want to know if I'm available for a high-level briefing. "Dr. Reese, I have the Pulitzer committee chair on the line." With time to read and reflect during my sabbatical, surely, I thought, the original ideas that gained me recognition would come pouring out with increasing speed. Let's go! My time is limited, and the days are slipping by. This break will end before I know it. The leaves on the trees outside the window at my home desk turned yellow and began to drop off. But the ideas were slow. I had high expectations for myself and wanted to plan something big, new, and original. In my head I imagined people saying, "He's had plenty of time to think about this—it had better be good!" But I wondered if I could do it.

In the story of Jacob, I see some of myself. In the early years, he was a goal-oriented man on the move and on the make—a Type A personality working at peak efficiency, a "highly effective person." Pursuing Rachel was one of his goals, and he worked hard to achieve it. After seven years of working for Laban, he married Leah in a last-minute "bait and switch." Seven more years were required for Laban's other daughter, Rachel (Gen 29). Then he worked hard to acquire enough resources to support his family. Now what? I didn't have to work seven years for a wife, but in my own case, each step of my professional life provided a goal and gave focus to my striving: work to get graduate degrees, check; six years on the road to promotion and tenure, check; five more years to the next rung of full professor, check; four more years and an appointment to an administrative post, check. Now what? I suppose I was at a crossroads, but why was that such a difficult challenge? Because secretly, I often prefer to have life distractions that keep me focused on the next goal ahead, without having to look within myself to see what I want to become. It's not easy to do that. I'm not the only one who gets used to having excuses for not achieving more than I do. If only I had time, I could (fill in the blank). If only I weren't so busy with teaching these classes, I could (blank). Well, during that time off I didn't have such excuses. Could I do something profound and special with my time, stepping back from the pace of career? Even in my sabbatical time, I was concerned with my productivity.

We all have a fundamental need to feel productive, to be employed toward a useful purpose, to pursue a passion, to be good stewards of our gifts. I can't say I had a major revelation during my reflections, and I know I will continue to be challenged to find my next goal within the professional world. But ultimately, of course, I know I'm called to keep it in proportion, to find my identity in who I am and *whose* I am, not in what I have or what position I hold. My sabbatical time was productive in giving me rest, a change of pace, and the chance to lay the groundwork for later writing. I was able to reflect in order to grow in new directions, even though at the time it didn't seem that much was happening. I did many other good things over that time. I went camping more often with my younger son, Daniel. I sat and did nothing, met with friends, went to lectures, and thought about some of the ideas in this book. The great literary figure Samuel Johnson has said, "All intellectual improvement arises from leisure." By the standards of modern culture, however, that's not a socially acceptable claim, so believing it required faith. My spiritual life raises the same issues. The time spent in prayer and meditation is productive time, even when little seems to happen. It prepares the way for growth.

Living a life that matters does not depend on measuring up to an occupational yardstick. Jacob knew he was on the road to success when he found the courage to return home and face Esau—for better or worse. He had his family now and all the material possessions he needed, telling Esau, "I have everything I want" (Gen 33:11). He still lacked reconciliation and peace. When he approached his brother in a spirit of wholeness and vulnerability, he was able to say that he could see "the face of God" (Gen 33:10). I want to be able to say that too. I would like to think my success comes in helping others, in having the many friends who have enriched my life, in seeing my boys grow up in ways that make me proud, in nurturing a marriage that brings me pleasure and intimacy, in being a part of a spiritual community, and in finding joy in a faith journey. I hope to learn as Jacob did that living a life of faith brings success far beyond mere productivity.

Notes

1. Richard Rohr, *Men and Women: The Journey of Spiritual Transformation* (St. Anthony Messenger Press, 1999) CD collection.

2. Harold Kushner, *Living a Life that Matters: Resolving the Conflict between Conscience and Success* (New York: A. A. Knopf, 2001).

Chapter 8

FATHERHOOD AS AN UNNATURAL ACT

But while he was still far off, his father saw him and was filled with compassion; he ran and put his arms around him and kissed him. (Luke 15:20)

This is my Father's world, a wanderer I may roam. Whate'er my lot, it matters not, My heart is still at home.[1]

When it comes to being a father, in my head I see myself as the wise dad in *Father Knows Best* or *My Three Sons*. My generation remembers those shows well, and they're still perennially available in reruns. That's a good thing considering the beating dads take in more recent television sitcoms like *Everybody Loves Raymond* and *Married with Children*, in which the fathers are selfish bumblers at best. I'm glad I saw the older, gentler models in my formative years. In those episodes, when something went wrong in the family or the kid tried to get away with something, the father always offered a solution to the problem, a kind word, and a wise insight. The father and son had a heart-to-heart moment, and all was well.

Perhaps the best example was *The Andy Griffith Show*, which has a large and devoted, now almost cult, following, even among my friends during college. My college English professor, Richard Kelly, wrote one of the many books analyzing the message behind the show's success. He pointed out that the strong and loving father-son relationship between Andy and Opie provided a model of family unity that extended to include the whole town of Mayberry. Across the many episodes, Andy's lessons to his son about sharing, friendship, honesty, and love shows the importance of those principles in shaping the life of a young man and in creating a healthy community. Even

Deputy Barney Fife acted the "son" to Sheriff Andy, who continued to love Barney in spite of his inevitable bumbling. Barney acknowledges that lesson of grace in an episode in which the deputy is reluctantly drawn into testifying about the sheriff's competence to remain in office: "You ask me if Andy runs a taut ship," Barney says. "No, he doesn't, but that's because of something he's been trying to teach me ever since I started working for him. And that is, when you're a lawman and dealing with people, you do a whole lot better if you go not so much by the book, but by the heart."[2] I try to be loving and wise with my two wonderful boys, but I haven't quite made it to Sheriff Andy's level. I don't know many men who have.

From a scriptural standpoint, the patriarchal language of fatherhood is a familiar way to think of God. As poet William Wordsworth said, "Father!— To God himself we cannot give a holier name!"[3] Jesus referred often to his "Father": "I must be in my Father's house," "My Father's house has many mansions," "Father, why hast thou forsaken me?" and, of course, in how he taught us to pray: "Our Father . . . ." God is a superfather. When our earthly parents fail, God is "Father to the Fatherless." The psalm says, "As a father has compassion on his children, so the Lord has compassion on those who fear him" (Ps 103:13). Although I try to avoid excessive use of gendered language for God in this book, it's easy to slip into it, especially when thinking about fatherhood. When describing God, the Bible uses the best qualities of fatherhood, but the actual fathers in the Bible are less than perfect, and there are many examples of broken relationships between father and son. Is anyone guilty of favoring one child over another? We learn in Genesis that Isaac's son Esau was a skillful hunter and a man of the field, while Jacob was a quiet man who lived in tents. Isaac loved Esau because he was fond of the game he caught, while Rebekah loved Jacob. Has anyone lost his temper at his children? King Saul, one of the bad guys of the Hebrew Bible, often did. In one case he became so angry with his son Jonathan that he cursed him and hurled his spear at him. Even a man after God's own heart, David, had a son named Absalom who became so estranged from his father that he staged a military coup.

It may seem odd to describe fatherhood as an unnatural act, but I would like to explore the idea. Of course, *becoming* a father is completely natural. *Exercising* fatherhood, however, the way God calls us to do, takes work and requires that we become better than we start out being. Theologian Kent Nerburn, in *Letters to My Son*, says, "This is not to say that becoming a father automatically makes you a good father. Fatherhood, like marriage, is a constant struggle against your limitations and self-interests. But the urge to be a perfect father is there, because your child is a perfect gift."[4]

Because so much of parenting is about our egos, good fatherhood is unnatural in the sense that it is not instinctual. Of course, we are filled with an unmistakable love for our children when they first come into our lives. They are extensions of ourselves; we bring them into being and give life to them, and for a long time they remain completely dependent on us. Our children may even look like us, with the same eyes or hair color. We feel a little like God, helping to create life. In fact, we may often be tempted to play God with our children by issuing commandments and reminding them of their total dependence on our care. For a time, we decide where our children go, what they do, and what they wear. We may seek to mold them in our image and treat them as extensions of ourselves.

Parenting gets harder as kids grow older. As a Darwinian adaptation, teenagers by necessity become harder to engage. If our children remained as loveable as when they are small, we could not bear to let go of them. The transition to adulthood for our kids must come, whether we're ready or not. I've watched my own children become more autonomous human beings with their own lives, hopes, and dreams. I faced the same transition when I was their age, and I know it's not always smooth. I recall riding in my parents' car one day as a child, needing an answer to a question that weighed on my mind—probably from reading too many fairy tales. I asked my parents, "When will I have go out to 'seek my fortune?'" It was done that way in the storybooks. I was relieved when my parents told me I could go whenever I was ready. The truth is, kids gladly tell their parents when they are ready, when they are independent human beings. For a dad, accepting and honoring that is an important but sometimes difficult step. I'm sure most fathers know how they want this passage to go, and I'm no exception. I want my children to share with me what is in their hearts, but as they become older they also naturally close off parts of themselves. They become more emotionally autonomous and may find it hard to share certain parts with their parents (the "mono-syllabic grunt phase"). If they show disrespect, it offends our egos, those parts of us that seek to control.

Even as we surrender some choices to our children, we continue to want them to do things as we would do them. It's easy to love our children when they are young and loveable. It also is easy to express love when we receive love in return, and young children are good at showing love on a basic level. Inevitably, however, as our children grow older, they gain a greater capacity to annoy us, to defy us, to act unlovingly toward us. That's when fatherhood gets more difficult and less "natural." As a call to discipleship, then, fatherhood calls us to be "unnatural," to venture outside ourselves and into a deeper expression of the kind of fatherhood God provides for us.

The ideal father role model in the Scriptures is in the familiar parable of the prodigal son. In a powerful illustration of God's love in Luke's Gospel, a father loves his sons but knows he can't hold on to them by force. The younger son asks for his share of the inheritance, takes it, and leaves for a far country. He eventually returns home. In this story, there is no evidence that the father favored one son over the other, even though it seems he had reason to do so. The older son did what was expected of him, a point of which he carefully reminded his father: "I have never disobeyed your command" (Luke 15:29). The prodigal, on the other hand, rejected the father before eventually coming home and seeking forgiveness. Through it all, the father kept loving both of his sons, but he is basically a stand-in for God. How can we measure up?

It's easy for a dad to give out love based on how well the relationship is going. When I perceive that I'm getting "an attitude" or "backtalk" from a teenager behaving normally, it is easy to withdraw and return the feeling in kind. That's when I must take a deep breath, extend the olive branch, say "I'm sorry" if I've been out of line, and reaffirm my love and my desire to understand. A transactional love, "I'll love you as long as you continue to do these things for me," is not selfless "agape" love, the highest form of love that we are commanded to have for others. For many years, the prodigal son's father got little back from their relationship. But the father obviously never stopped loving his son for a moment. Without waiting to see if the son would grovel for forgiveness, the Bible says that "*while he was still far off,* his father saw him and was filled with compassion; he ran and put his arms around him and kissed him" (Luke 15:20, my emphasis).

As my older son finished high school, we shared the difficult process of deciding, as I jokingly put it, what college "we" would attend the next fall. The summer before his senior year, we traveled all over the country to see colleges: ten in all, counting his hometown school, my own employer. We had it down to a science. My wife helped organize the itinerary, doing such a good job that I only had to take out my file folder when we got off the plane. "Mom says we're supposed to proceed out of terminal B, turn right and walk fifty yards to board the blue shuttle bus to the Avis counter." I also owe her a lot for helping me think big about college. I remember asking her how in the world she expected us to be able to afford some of the colleges our son considered. I secretly suspected it might come down to either my driving a new car or paying for tuition, but she encouraged our son to apply to the best places he thought appropriate—and I came around to agreeing. On one of our many visits, as we left a campus that Aaron found appealing, he asked me, "Dad, do you think we can afford this place?" I said, "You just work on finding the place that's right for you, and let Mom and me worry about the rest." That felt better to me, more like the father I wanted to be.

Later, as we got on each other's nerves during the application process, he got frustrated with us for constantly monitoring his deadlines for scholarships, applications, and so forth. I could understand how he felt. I realized that it had become the main content of our interaction together, and it was getting old. He would say in exasperation, "It's being taken care of!" At one such moment, I had to make the effort to go into his room, sit on the bed, and talk with him about it (in what I hoped would be a "father-knows-best moment"). I said I would try to go easier on the checkups and understood how that could get old, but that basically his mother and I simply wanted to be involved in this decision and in his life—not to check to see if he had or would screw up, but because we loved him. We wanted to be included in his life, to participate with him, to have an intimacy based on shared experience. I said I knew I couldn't play his game for him, but I at least wanted to know what time the game started so I could be there to cheer him on. How often do we think of God as a superfather—checking up on us to see how we're doing on the rules? What God actually wants is a deep, intimate relationship with us, to be involved in our circumstances, for us to open our lives to him as we share our hopes and fears and allow him to bless us.

Eventually, college decision time rolled around. For a number of reasons, I thought Aaron would be better off at one university, while all indications showed that he was strongly considering choosing another. There was a real risk that he would not do what I wanted! Like a typical eighteen-year-old, he felt I was nagging him. Like a typical father, I wanted to be able to control the situation, to dictate the choice that I thought was best for him. I was surprised by how much I had become invested in the outcome of the process.

Looking back on my own experience at Aaron's age, I know I simply fell into many decisions about my college experience from lack of awareness and imagination. The process then was not nearly as high-pressured and competitive as it seems today. I simply knew I wanted to get away from home and go, if not to a "far country," at least a fair drive down the interstate. If a college offered a reasonably attractive brochure, it was a candidate. I didn't want Aaron to repeat the same mistakes. Given my profession and its academic yardsticks of prestige, it's easy for me to look back and wish I could fine-tune my biography, that my resume included a prestigious undergraduate institution. Now was my chance vicariously to rewrite that period of my life.

But I'm not Aaron's boss; I'm his dad. He would have to do all the work at the school he chose, not I. We talked about it, and I did my best to give him good advice as a dad. I still didn't opt out of sharing my point of view. I owed him that. I wrote occasional e-mails to let him know I was proud of him, that he was going to be successful regardless of the outcome, and that we loved him no matter what. In addition, I let him know that he was part of my spiritual life, that I was praying for him, that God would lead him to choose a school where he could make the best use of his gifts, that we as his parents would also be guided in giving him wise counsel and support. I knew that no matter how independent he acted on the outside, he faced a big decision as he stepped out of the familiar family space.

I remembered how I used to drop him off at kindergarten every morning. Although the other parents dropped their kids off at the front to walk in by themselves, he always liked me to park the car and go in with him. Some of the other parents, I heard from the teacher, were curious about it, but I didn't mind and even liked doing it. We had a little extra time together while he got situated, and then I said my goodbyes and slipped off without making a big deal about it. Eventually, of course, when the time was right, I stopped going in. And now, all these years later, we navigated a different transition between the comfort zone of the familiar and new challenges, and it was my job to help prepare him for them. My wife often reminds me that teenagers need "roots and wings." When the prodigal son was away, something planted deep inside from his father probably gave him roots—the idea that he could return home—even while he was equipped to leave. The Bible says, "He came to himself." Wherever he was and however old he got, he was still part of the family.

As much as I enjoyed being a dad to those cute little boys, who were once totally dependent on the Dad-god, I've enjoyed just as much seeing them become their own selves. I see those same personalities, just in bigger packages. I love having them give their dad a hand when we camp or travel, offer advice about my computer, or provide tips on working some other electronic device. I see the truth of the promise in Proverbs: "Train a child in the way he should go, and when he is old he will not depart from it" (22:6). I know I can trust that, and I'm proud of what my young men are becoming.

Sometimes when I look at my older son, who is a bit taller than I am, it's hard to remember that I could once hold a little boy on my lap without breaking my leg. And now I've got two of them who could inflict that kind of injury. But the "little boy" is still in both of them, as it is in me and in every man, still earnestly desiring a father's love (and desiring *the* Father's love). That's what the prodigal learned in the parable: that he still needed his father's love and that it was still there, an enthusiastic, running-to-meet-him, unconditional love.

We all need to learn that lesson, especially as men, when the roles reverse and our turn arrives to be that kind of father. Not every man has kids of his own, and not all men who do can be with their children the way they desire. Jobs, separations, ex-wives, and breaches of all kinds build barriers to being an active dad. But we can all be a father figure to someone. In that role, do we treat our "children" as something else to manage and control, to compete through and shape in our own image? Are we reluctant to be vulnerable with them and speak from the heart for fear of looking foolish? Do we wish to hide the fact that we're not always going to get it right? We need to crack through that wall. Admitting we're human won't damage our credibility with our children, as long as we commit to being in relationship with them, giving and seeking forgiveness. I don't think they mind if we speak honestly about our spiritual doubts and admit we don't have all the answers. None of us do, but that doesn't always keep us from wanting to be "god" in our households. Should we feel tempted to play that role, however, let it be the kind of god father in the parable, so we can at least show our children a glimpse of how God wants it to be. As Wendell Berry puts it,

And this, then,
is the vision of that Heaven of which
we have heard, where those who love
each other have forgiven each other,
where, for that, the leaves are green
the light a music in the air,
all is unentangled,
and all is undismayed[5]

Notes

1. "This Is My Father's World," words by Maltbie D. Babcock, 1901, traditional English melody arr. Franklin L. Sheppard, 1915.

2. Richard Kelly, *The Andy Griffith Show* (Winston-Salem NC: John F. Blair Publisher, 1981).

3. William Wordsworth, "Sponsors," in *The Complete Poetical Works*, Ecclesiastical Sonnets, part 3 (London: Macmillan and Co., 1888; Bartleby.com, 1999) http://www.bartleby.com/145/ww668.html.

4. Kent Nerburn, *Letters to My Son: A Father's Wisdom on Manhood, Life, and Love* (Novato CA: New World Library, 1999) 173.

5. Wendell Berry, "To My Mother," from *The Selected Poems of Wendell Berry* (Berkeley CA: Counterpoint Press, 1998) 161.

Chapter 9

THE GIFT OF PRESENCE

Whoever wishes to be great among you must be your servant, and whoever wishes to be first among you must be your slave; just as the Son of Man came not to be served but to serve . . . . (Matthew 20:26-28)

Let the same mind be in you that was in Christ Jesus, who, though he was in the form of God, did not regard equality with God as something to be exploited, but emptied himself, taking the form of a slave. (Philippians 2:5-7)

Brother, let me be your servant; let me be as Christ to you. Pray that I might have the grace to let you be my servant, too. ("The Servant Song")[1]

Modern society runs on the principles of power and control. When we operate in hierarchical institutions, many of them large and impersonal, getting ahead often means thinking of others as cogs in the machine, as means to our ends. But that's contrary to a spiritually guided way of working and living. If we are to avoid separating the life of work from the daily faith journey, we must find a way for faith to guide all our relationships, no matter where we find them. I know I'm supposed to be kind and fair to others, treat them as I would like to be treated, and be a decent human being. Most of us, I hope, have a basic sense of correct behavior and many even a streak of altruism. We don't need a spiritual life or theological understanding to conform to basic social norms. However, beyond those basics, principles of faith have found their way into recent thinking about how to work with people, especially in large organizations.

Although these principles are rooted in a number of faith traditions, some important philosophies of leadership and management have expanded particularly from the gospel message of servanthood. Jesus claimed the role of a servant and preached the paradox that "the first shall be last." "The Servant Song," quoted above, begins, "Brother, let me be your servant." In his 1970 book, *The Servant as Leader*, influential business consultant Robert Greenleaf offered guidance for the aspiring professional: "It begins with the natural feeling that one wants to serve, to serve first. Then conscious choice brings one to aspire to lead. The best test is: do those served grow as persons; do they, while being served, become healthier, wiser, freer, more autonomous, more likely themselves to become servants?"[2]

In my experience at a university, faculty members are deeply suspicious of anyone who aspires to be an "administrator." Often the only way to get such a job is not to want it. In Greenleaf's paradigm, great leaders are experienced by their followers as servants. Coercion and control are less oppressive in institutions more devoted to serving their members, in which a more humane approach helps legitimate the power of the leaders. Greenleaf's ideas have influenced leadership gurus like Stephen Covey, author of the bestseller *Seven Habits of Highly Effective People*.[3] One of Covey's servant-oriented quotations is "Seek first to understand, then to be understood." Now popularized so widely in the secular world, these concepts echo the spiritual principle in St. Francis's familiar "Peace Prayer": "Lord, make me an instrument of thy peace." The prayer goes on to say, "Grant that I may not so much seek to be consoled as to console; *to be understood, as to understand.*" Tom Cruise popularized a more modern expression of a servant slogan in his title role in the movie *Jerry McGuire*, in which a struggling sports agent tries to help a temperamental football player client.[4] Jerry reaches something of a breakthrough in his difficult relationship with an athlete when he finally repeats the plea, "Help *me* help *you!*"

Every year brings new "best practices" for managers and leaders, but by their nature, these principles must be firmly rooted in our spiritual lives if they are to be effective. They are a life choice and can't be tried on temporarily for the purpose of getting things done. The beauty of the servant principle is that, while there is less room at the peak of the traditional power pyramid and it is "lonely at the top," there is no limit to the number of people who can serve. Jesus says if anyone wants to follow him, there is plenty of room. That doesn't mean becoming a martyr or an ascetic, renouncing all earthly pleasures, but it does lead us to be more open to the humanity of others and give priority to their needs. It's not always easy to serve, especially when demands for results, actions, and plans pressure us. We're cogs too. Stepping out of that box takes courage and imagination and faith to see that the entire community grows as a result.

To live the servant principle requires "being" as much as "doing." The WWJD bracelets that many wear pose the question, What would Jesus do? I suppose that's not a bad place to start in thinking like a servant, even though I dislike what seem like hokey religious gimmicks. But the "Servant Song" adds another line: "Brother, let me be your servant, let me be as Christ to you." What does that mean? What does it mean to "be as Christ"? A few years ago, I felt moved to pursue a program in my church called Stephen Ministry, which has helped me understand that question better. The program provides a caring outreach to those in crisis, which can include death of a loved one, divorce, loss of job, or terminal illness. I suppose I've always been interested in psychology, and I had the benefit myself of a wise pastoral counselor. Much of what I did in my job involved some form of counseling, so I thought I might have something to offer.

After several weeks of training, I began meeting with the first of the men with whom I'd be paired for weekly visits. These one-on-one relationships continue until closed by mutual agreement, and whatever we talk about remains confidential. In addition to the visits, I would meet twice a month with other caregivers to assess how best to carry out our work. Reflecting on some years of experience now, I see that often I have not felt as effective as I wished in working with "care receivers." Some have hope of recovering from their crisis, whether finding a job or healing from a broken relationship; those with terminal illness will not. I can't fix them, and often I can only listen. I may feel that I must be something to them that I am not. Professionals train for years to deliver counseling and treat mental and physical ailments. Social workers are available to help those in need. What, then, can I possibly contribute? I must remind myself of why I'm really there. In thinking of my personal need for reassurance and renewal, I recall singing the "Servant Song" at church one Sunday. It stuck with me because it seemed to embody the spirit we are called to live as disciples, in particular through the Stephen Ministry.

Brother, let me be your servant; let me be as Christ to you.
　Pray that I might have the grace to let you be my servant, too.
We are pilgrims on a journey; we are brothers on the road.
　We are here to help each other walk the mile and bear the load.

I will hold the Christ-light for you in the nighttime of your fear.
  I will hold my hand out to you; speak the peace you long to hear.
I will weep when you are weeping; when you laugh, I'll laugh with you.
  I will share your joy and sorrow till we've seen this journey through.
When we sing to God in heaven, we shall find such harmony
  Born of all we've known together of Christ's love and agony.[5]

I have been taught, but sometimes find difficult to believe, that we all
have something extraordinarily special to contribute: the gift of presence.
The words to the hymn don't say, "Let me be a psychiatrist to you" or "Let
me be an employment counselor to you" or "Let me be a therapist." They
say, "Let me be as *Christ* to you." If I look at it that way, I realize how much
people hunger for that kind of relationship and what a tremendous role I am
called to play in their lives. As much as we spend time each day talking to
others, how often do we truly listen? It's a rare commodity, especially for
men, who often talk to gain advantage or polish an image. I've seen the gift
of my time and a willing ear make a difference. Now I am continually
reminded of that truth.

I hadn't seen my friend Hoye for a while. I had met him about ten years
earlier when he was in his eighties and long since retired. He was a gentle
soul and always sat toward the front of the church. His daughter or son
drove him there after his wife died, but I hadn't seen him there lately, and it
had been a few years since I visited him at his retirement home apartment.
Hoye had always greatly encouraged me, as he did many others. A lot of
people his age give up on doing much. Some of the other residents (he called
them "the inmates") spent their time complaining—but not Hoye. He was
computer savvy and helped the others send e-mails to relatives, a simple service that sometimes brought and kept families together. He had a business
card listing his phone number, e-mail address, and this message: "No matter
the time of night or day, may I help in any way?"

One day, a mutual friend called me and said Hoye didn't have much
time to live, but that he expressly said he wanted to see me. He was saying
his goodbyes, and I was deeply touched that he included me on his list. But
what do you say to someone who is about to die? I was unsure what I would
find when I knocked on his door. What would he look like, what would we
talk about, would I be intruding on a difficult, private time? I realized, even
in my apprehension, that I didn't have to say anything. I simply had to go
and be there, to let him know that we were still friends, to shake his hand
and listen to him. Toward the end of our visit, I asked Hoye if he wanted me

to pray with him, and he said, "Oh, I wish we could pray." Praying out loud was not part of my faith routine growing up, but in recent years I do it more often, including prayer as a vital part of my Stephen Ministry visits. It seems to help guys in particular to "cut through the crap," to get real fast and zero in on exactly what's in their hearts. With practice, prayer comes with greater ease, of course, so as Hoye and I held hands and bowed our heads, I thanked God for his life, his spirit of service, and the many lives he had touched, asking that he would be filled with a deep sense of peace as he confronted the end. I admired his spirit then and now as he sought to approach the end of life with dignity and openness about his feelings. I felt honored that he called on me at that time—not to do anything more than to be present, to be in relationship with him. Stephen Ministry helped teach me that.

For us to be the body of Christ, we must be in right relationship with each other. That means giving and receiving: "Pray that I might have the grace *to let you be my servant too.*" My friend was a great servant, but now he knew he needed to gather support from his friends. This principle is brought home to me especially in the occasional service of foot washing at our church, and in many Christian denominations, on Maundy Thursday before Easter. The pastors kneel before those who come forward one by one and symbolically wipe their shoes with a towel. It is disconcerting to sit in the receiving role, and I often recall how Peter at first recoiled at the prospect of allowing Jesus to wash him. Why is such a practice so profoundly moving? Because in that powerful moment we participate in the two-way blessing of allowing ourselves to be served as well as to serve, something Christ modeled for the disciples. We are expected to love and to receive love, to love without the condition that we be loved in return, and to receive love without the expectation that it be given. When this body of believers works as it should, we have the power to be as Christ to others, to bring them into a community of wholeness.

The Hebrew Bible commands us to love God, but in the Gospels, loving God and loving neighbor are more emphatically linked. When a lawyer, seeking to test Jesus, asked him how to get eternal life, Jesus asked him what was written. "'You shall love the Lord our God with all your heart, and with all your soul, and with all your strength, and with all your mind; and your neighbor as yourself.' And he said to him, 'You have given the right answer; do this, and you will live'" (Luke 10:27).

I think that Jesus, knowing the man wasn't sincerely motivated to know the answer, allowed himself some sarcasm at the end—"Right, just go do that." Jesus understood that it was easier said than done, emphasizing this connection further in his response elsewhere to the question of a more sincerely motivated scribe:

> "Of all the commandments, which is the most important?" "The most important one," answered Jesus, "is this: 'Hear, O Israel, the Lord our God, the Lord is one. Love the Lord your God with all your heart and with all your soul and with all your mind and with all your strength.' [The second is this: 'Love your neighbor as yourself.' There is no commandment greater than these." "Well said, teacher," the man replied. "You are right in saying that God is one and there is no other but him. To love him with all your heart, with all your understanding and with all your strength, and to love your neighbor as yourself is more important than all burnt offerings and sacrifices." When Jesus saw that he had answered wisely, he said to him, "You are not far from the kingdom of God." (Mark 12:28-34)

I sense Jesus here saying, "You are so *close*. If only others could see as you seem to see, if they can just change their thinking to see beyond the many restrictions placed on the law to the infinitely liberating power that it can unleash. You are almost there."

It's a simple reemphasis in a way, but it opens an entirely new way of thinking. John wrote something like that: "Dear friends, I am not writing a new commandment, for it is an old one you have always had, right from the beginning. This commandment—to love one another—is the same message you heard before. Yet it is also new" (1 John 2:1-17).

That's what the gospel means to me: not a bunch of new rules to go with the previous Ten Commandments, but a reemphasis on the power of love. We are called into life, into the inner spirit of the Law. I often feel the need for this liberating force, even at home with my own family—the ones I should have the least difficulty loving. When my older son, the first to leave the nest, went away to college, I missed him deeply. Before he left and during brief weekend visits home that first year, I found myself a little resentful of his friends with whom he spent so much time—time that I wanted for myself. Wasn't I entitled to that time? After all, I'm his dad. I may feel like I deserve some kind of medal for being willing to support the high cost of his college education. But didn't my own father do the same for me, and didn't his father do what he could for him without any thought of repayment? If I'm not careful, at work I can become resentful that an adversary may receive something to which I don't think she's entitled. I can even get a little jealous of colleagues who earn more money than I do. That's why I need to remember the old commandments in a new way, to become more fully alive in God, and to have the love of God spilling out of me into the lives of others. I need to stop rationing it out and instead allow them to be fully alive as well. I like John Shelby Spong's wording, that to follow Christ is to love "wastefully."[6]

I watched my dad during the last years of his life loyally caring for my stepmother, who suffered from Alzheimer's disease. With declining memory, each moment for her became a new day, not connected to the past or future. During one visit home, before the illness took too great a toll, I realized that I could greet her cheery "good morning" each time I passed through the kitchen where she sat eating as though it were the first time. For my dad, I thought it must be particularly tough to show kindness, or to do anything, without knowing if she would remember it a moment later—or if she even knew who he was. Her world had shrunk completely into the present. One time, perhaps during that same visit, I ate with her at the kitchen table, just the two of us. By then we all knew it was pointless to carry on a conventional conversation with her, since regular chats often refer to what has happened or is about to happen. Instead, at one point I felt led to say, "I sure am having a good time here with you." Her face brightened, and she said, "I am too!" At that point it was enough to seize that moment and enjoy it, to express it, and "be" in it.

I always enjoyed the movie *Groundhog Day*, with Bill Murray playing the guy who seemed destined to relive the same day over and over.[7] Every morning he wakes up at the same time, on the same day, to the same song on the clock radio, and hears the same comments from the people he meets. Once the next replay begins, no one except him has any recollection of the day's events. I realize better now that the film has a deep and intricate spiritual message. Phil, Murray's character, begins the story as a self-centered, arrogant, unattached weathercaster. After countless iterations of that one day, however, he finally begins to grow—no longer taking advantage of his prior knowledge to manipulate and ingratiate. Instead, he learns to take delight in using his knowledge to serve others. With his own growing understanding of the needs of the people in that town, he grows in his ability to serve. The irony, of course, is that no one has any memory of his service beyond each day. He has to be motivated by the simple desire to serve for its own sake, not to store up credits for himself. The whole town has Alzheimer's with respect to anything beyond Groundhog Day. One analysis of the film suggests that Phil is God of that town in the sense of his omniscience about what will happen, but more aptly he is Christ to that town. Bill Murray makes an unlikely Christ figure, but his character effectively has to be as Christ in order to escape the cycle in which he is trapped. As a result, he becomes someone truly lovable.

I want to be a better servant, whether in the roles of daily life or in the Stephen Ministry, which after all is simply a microcosm of the way to do it anywhere. Just because I've received training doesn't mean it always comes naturally, but it has made me more mindful at least of trying, if not always succeeding, to be more attentive to others, especially to my family. After all, if I'm willing to take time to listen to the problems of someone I haven't known before, how can I not try to do the same at home? I'm grateful that the more formal relationships set up through this ministry challenge me to carry my desire to connect into all my encounters: being as Christ to my enemy, not concerned with how he or she may be rewarded; being as Christ to my friends, not envying their achievements but celebrating with them; being as Christ to my children, teaching them and letting them move on to new lives apart from me; being as Christ to those I care for, speaking "the peace they long to hear." We don't have the luxury of practicing every Groundhog Day over and over again until we get it right. But we do find ourselves in roles that call for servant leaders, whether at home or in the many organizations and institutions in which we are involved. It is within our power to be more generous with ourselves, to *do* and to *be*, to share our gift of presence.

Notes

1. "The Servant Song," words and music by Richard Gillard, 1977.

2. Robert Greenleaf, *The Servant Leader Within: A Transformative Path* (Mahwah NJ: Paulist Press, 2003) 29.

3. Stephen Covey, *The 7 Habits of Highly Effective People: Restoring the Character Ethic* (New York: Free Press, 2004).

4. *Jerry Maguire*, written and dir. Cameron Crowe, Gracie Films, 1996.

5. "The Servant Song."

6. John Shelby Spong, *Eternal Life: A New Vision* (New York: Harper Collins, 2009).

7. *Groundhog Day*, dir. Harold Ramis, screenplay by Danny Rubin and Harold Ramis, Columbia Pictures Corporation, 1993.

Chapter 10

UNSPOKEN WORDS OF LOVE

So we do not lose heart. Even though our outer nature is wasting away, our inner nature is being renewed day by day. (2 Corinthians 4:16)

One of the saddest things at a funeral service is hearing the minister brought in for the occasion say, "I didn't know (name of deceased) very well." That either means the guy didn't show up at church often or that no one was available who truly did "know" the person. I don't want that to happen to me. For my own selfish reasons, if nothing else, I want the person talking about me to say I was known, really known. It would even be a great honor for me to have my sons feel up to the task, to be able to say, "I knew this guy, my dad, and I'm going to tell you a little about him." A newspaper financial column called "Give Kids a Parting Gift" urged parents to tell their adult children the whereabouts of their wills, bank accounts, safety deposit keys, and names of their doctors. That's a considerate idea and typical of the many ways we are urged to put our affairs in order to help our loved ones when we're gone. But far more important is the greater gift of leaving them with the knowledge of how much we loved them and how much they meant to us. Why is it often hard for so many people—especially men—to express themselves to those with whom we live most closely? Reba McEntire, in her heartbreaking song about a child's distant father, expresses a far too common experience: "The greatest man I never knew lived just down the hall / And every day we said hello but never touched at all . . . / I never really knew him and now it seems so sad / Everything he gave to us took all he had."[1] Too many dads have a hard time expressing who they are and how they feel about their kids, which is what children want most to hear.

Losing a parent always confronts us with deep questions, and at the time of the loss we think through some of them better than we do others. For men, no matter how old we are, losing a father has a special impact. Growing up, and well into our adulthood, we long for our dads to have confidence in us, to have faith that we can make our way in the world. When my own father died, I wanted to prepare a eulogy for his memorial service, but I wasn't sure I should take on a speaking role when the power of fresh emotions might result in something unpredictable. Still, I thought I could do it as a gift for my dad, my brother and sister, and our family friends. A word from the heart means a lot at a time like that, but I also had a deeper motivation. I needed a gift of feeling that I had a better understanding of my dad and how he felt about me. Did he love me? Was he proud of me? Every father has different ways of showing these feelings, so we all need to answer such questions for ourselves. The function of a eulogy in a service is to say something, hopefully not too exaggerated, about the enduring positive qualities of the loved one and to express the loss felt by the community. I didn't have any formal structure in mind. I just knew I wanted to say something from the heart that would resonate with others. I needed to reflect on who my dad really was and what he meant to me and those who knew him. My eulogy assignment would give me a way to do that.

Although we always wish for more time, my dad lived a full life. We had helped him celebrate his eightieth birthday the previous year. We enjoyed a wonderful party planned by my musician brother with our dad's favorite music performed by family and friends. I flew up to be the emcee and give him an affectionate "roast." He, in turn, quipped to the group at the end that he had hoped for a money tree as a gift—but realized his friends were so cheap they would have a hard time getting the coins to stick on! Dad had a good sense of humor, and I teased him at our last Christmas together about his "Body Recall" exercise class at church. I told some visitors that Dad showed up for Body Recall, but it turned out he was out of warranty! My words were an unfortunate prophecy when he landed in the hospital not long afterward.

He had heart surgery that seemed to go well, but complications developed a few weeks later. He went back to the hospital, had another operation, and stayed there. After a few days, my sister called to say he wasn't doing well. Always the sharp mind, my former college professor dad now showed signs of confusion, seeing things in the hospital room that weren't there, including an odd sighting of a "man with a hat." I hadn't thought until then that his illness was serious enough to justify getting off work and taking the long flight to be there, but I talked about it with my wife and we quickly agreed that I should go as soon as possible. I wasn't sure what was in store, but I had plenty of time to think about it as I took that plane trip alone to Knoxville.

Picturing my dad in a hospital bed, where neither he nor I had ever lain before, made me uncomfortable. Part of it, I'm sure, is that I saw my own future, and that vision made me anxious and apprehensive. As we get older, it's especially hard for men to think about becoming less independent and more reliant on others. The parent becomes a child. I thought about the passage at the end of John's Gospel, where Jesus says to Peter, "Very truly, I tell you, when you were younger, you used to fasten your own belt and to go wherever you wished. But when you grow old, you will stretch out your hands, and someone else will fasten a belt around you and take you where you do not wish to go" (John 21:18).

I don't know about other guys, but that scares the hell out of me. I wondered whether I could trust God's presence in these circumstances. On the plane, I didn't feel much like reading, so I used the time to write some thoughts. I prayed, if not for a cure, then for healing and wholeness and peace, for my dad and for those surrounding him. I prayed that God would speak to me and that I would be available to hear what God had to say. As events unfolded and I tried to listen, God did have a message of comfort and reassurance that eventually found its way into my eulogy.

My brother met me at the airport—just as he had when I was called home years earlier after our mom died—and took me to Dad's house to spend the night before we visited him in the hospital the next day. When I arrived at Dad's room the next morning, I saw how serious his condition was. He had aged ten years in the few months since our Christmas visit. I could barely understand him, and he had difficulty eating. Doctors attributed the "confusion" to the disorientation that comes from long hospital stays, but that didn't sound right to us. Later it was discovered that he had suffered mild strokes, and a staph infection had set in.

He was in bad shape, and it hurt to see it—especially for a man who had valued his privacy and dignity so much. Hospital staff, no matter how well intentioned, come and go without much regard for the patient's personal space. As the next days passed, I didn't see how he could go home anytime soon, and I knew I couldn't stay much longer. There were questions concerning weeks of intravenous treatment to counter infection, living wills (which fortunately he had), Do-Not-Resuscitate orders, and feeding tubes, which I knew he didn't want. One night I tried with great difficulty to help him take a sip of water. In his frustration and my own, I felt utterly defeated, helpless, and pierced to my soul that I was unable to render better care to my own father. I placed a photo of him on the room's bulletin board, a picture of him in better health with a big smile. If I couldn't be there, I wanted visitors to see a different man than the one lying in that bed.

As I anticipated the possibility of my dad's death and my desire to understand better who he really was, I was drawn to Paul's second letter to the Corinthians. Paul has something to say about the inner man and the outer man.

> So, we do not lose heart. Even though our outer nature is wasting away, our inner nature is being renewed day by day . . . because we look not at what can be seen but at what cannot be seen; for what can be seen is temporary, but what cannot be seen is eternal. For we know that if the earthly tent we live in is destroyed, we have a building from God, a house not made with hands, eternal in the heavens. For in this tent we groan, longing to be clothed with our heavenly dwelling . . . . For while we are still in this tent, we groan under our burden, because we wish not to be unclothed but to be further clothed, so that what is mortal may be swallowed up by life. . . . So, if anyone is in Christ, there is a new creation: everything old has passed away; see, everything has become new! (2 Cor 4:16–5:4; 5:17)

I took a portable stereo from the house, and when I played some of Dad's favorite music I heard him humming along. Now that he lay in the hospital bed and was unable to change the subject, I took advantage of him and told him exactly how I felt—that I loved him. Then, not long after, as I sat next to the bed on a sunny Sunday afternoon, he did something to resolve all of the medical uncertainties. He died. In the next few moments, the hospital staff disconnected the tubes, turned off the machines, and left me alone in the room with my dad's "tent." Dignity and quiet returned. The room became sacred ground.

The paradox of the Christian faith, in my familiar theme, is that God's power is made perfect in weakness; while the outer man wastes away, the inner man struggles to be born. The part of us that is eternal grows as we enter into an intimate relationship with our Creator, even as the part of us that is transient must inevitably get weaker. In Dad's last days, I witnessed the outer man wasting away before my eyes. Although it is hard to watch our outer bodies decline in vigor and reliability, we have confidence that our inner nature is renewed day by day. The inner man becomes stronger until it finally bursts forth. That birth, just as in childbirth, comes with groaning and pain, but the result is new life, and I had a powerful sense of it in the holy ground of that hospital room, of the strange, paradoxical mystery of dying into life.

With those thoughts in mind, I returned with my family to the home-town church for Dad's memorial a few weeks later, ready to be in community and celebrate a life, to give thanks to God for all of our lives, for the abundant life. I thought about how best to understand what I had expe-rienced and express it in the form of a eulogy. The day before the service, I went to the large Gothic-style sanctuary to prepare myself for my talk. I wanted to do a good job in this important mission. With no one around, I took the opportunity to stand at the large, ornate pulpit and get comfortable in that space. I rehearsed my words, gazing out at the familiar space in the cool half-darkness, with the late afternoon sun barely penetrating the stained-glass windows. I wanted to visualize exactly how it would feel to stand there and look out at friends and family. I thought about the wed-dings, baptisms, and other important moments in my life that had taken place in that church.

I particularly remembered coming to the same sanctuary for a memorial service for my mother, who died suddenly and unexpectedly twenty-five years earlier on New Year's Eve. A lot of time elapsed between these two pow-erful losses—half my lifetime. I experienced them differently. With more emotional and spiritual water under the bridge, I was now able to reflect on the loss of my dad from a different place and at a different level. After my mom died, the family met around the kitchen table, which had always been her command center, to plan the service. I remember in my grief and anger wanting to have it be *my* moment, to be allowed to stew in my suffering. I wanted the service to be an expression of my personal pain, with minimal involvement from the congregation. One of our pastors gently admonished me that it was about others too, that they were also hurting and needed to participate, that the time was for the entire community to come together in a reaffirmation of faith. I remember entering early from the side door and taking my seat with my dad and younger brother and sister in the front of the sanctuary reserved for the "family," lost in my thoughts as I listened to the service. When it was over, we prepared to move to the front to receive friends. I stood up and looked behind me for the first time to discover a sea of faces I had not realized were there. At that moment and in the loving touches, smiles, and tears that followed, I had a powerful sense of being part of that community and coming together as the body of Christ. To grief was added a feeling of gratitude that I could gather with them in that place and draw strength from the power of community. Returning now to the same church to remember my dad, I came more in a spirit of celebration and inclusion with the full realization that I came together with a faith community to remember a loved one. I wanted to celebrate Dad's life, but also our lives and life itself: the abundant life, shaken together, pressed down, running over. In doing that, I wanted to capture in words something of the real man—the inner man.

My dad was a man of his generation, much like his own father, and I wasn't surprised to hear one of Dad's surgeons refer to him as stoic. He enjoyed life, his family, and friends, but he wasn't given to expressing deep introspection—at least not to me. To help him along, we gave him a book one Christmas called *Grandfather Remembers*, which provided a number of structuring questions and plenty of blank space for answering them. No luck. The book's pages remained pristinely blank for years afterward, unmarred by recollections. We eventually followed through with a threat to sit him down with a tape recorder for an interrogation and not let him up until we collected at least a few stories. Unlike the style of younger men these days, his reserve led him to prefer handshakes over hugs with me in my adulthood, until my wife goaded us into the latter. If I started getting too "in touch" with my feelings around him, he usually changed the subject: "How's the weather in Texas?" Although I think I understand better now, I found that frustrating. At least it opened up more possibilities for conversation when he got the Weather Channel!

Men of my generation have been encouraged to be more open about our inner lives, and I am more outwardly emotional than my dad. Around ten years old or so, I was caught in some mischief with a classmate and sent to the principal's office. For my ne'er-do-well friend, the trip was routine, but a good boy like me wasn't used to being on the wrong side of the authorities. Embarrassed and angry about my predicament and the shame of it all, I felt my eyes fill with tears. The assistant principal, ironically a woman, said, "Come on, Stephen, be a man." She meant, I suppose, that I should control my emotions, as a man would—a man like, for example, my father. I never saw him cry, even following the death of my mother. At the time, I remember both marveling about it and feeling troubled by it. I didn't understand how my dad could restrain himself so successfully as he faced a steady stream of grieving friends and relatives who came to our home when the news spread. One of my dad's best friends was among those who arrived with food and sympathy. "Griff" was a big bear of a man, so likeable that he was the only one my mom ever allowed to smoke in the house. When he came to visit, he went straight to the lower kitchen cabinet where he knew she always hid a yellow glass ashtray just for him. Now, the two of us stepped out front in the sunshine of a cold January morning to escape the noisy house, and I confessed what I had observed. In an insight best provided by my dad's peer, he said something I needed to hear: that my dad was no doubt crying deep inside where no one but him could see.

As a man of his generation, Dad didn't share his personal troubles with his children. I'm sure he was lonely after our mother's death, but we had our own lives, and he probably didn't want to burden us. I knew he had faced other challenges in recent years, including health concerns, but again he didn't want us to worry about him. It wasn't his style. For a man of his generation, that was the loving thing to do—to shoulder his duty and be strong on behalf of the family. Nor was it his style to dictate what we should do in our lives; those were our decisions. But actions speak louder than words, and he let us know in his actions that he was there to support us in whatever we decided to do. The way we spend our time and our resources says a lot, and reflecting back, I see that Dad's actions spoke for him in ways I didn't appreciate at the time.

While living at home for a quarter during college, I jogged on a highway near the campus late one night after work. It was close to midnight when I finished and realized I'd locked my keys in the car. I felt foolish and knew it was late, but I didn't see any way around calling home and sheepishly asking for help. After a short while my dad pulled up, silently got out of the car, unlocked my door, got back in his car, and drove off. No words were needed, so he didn't use any. He may have been angry, put out, or aggravated; I don't know, but that's not the point. He came and provided what I needed. I could count on him.

Nevertheless, I always dreaded looking foolish in front of my dad, and I went to great lengths to avoid it. Not long after getting married, I wanted to buy a larger house for my growing family but knew we couldn't afford it yet, especially with prices rising rapidly in our area. I proposed a scheme to keep and rent out our first house while assuming the seller's mortgage for the new one, with Dad loaning me a considerable amount of money to make up the sale price. I would repay it in a few years and, in the meantime, give him a lien on the property and monthly interest-only payments. I was convinced that rapidly rising real-estate values made the deal a no-brainer for him and for me. I would simply refinance in a few years and pay him back with money to spare. I even had a big-shot daydream about buying him an expensive watch with the profits from my business savvy. However, soon after, the bottom fell out of the market and it was tough to keep up our payments to him. Neither house was worth enough to sell or refinance. I would have given anything not to renege on our agreement; Dad had warned me about the dangers of loaning money to friends and family. But I was so convinced I was right, and, after all, I was now a mature, responsible adult. Finally, I didn't see an alternative. On one of Dad's visits, I swallowed my embarrassment, told him I needed to talk with him, and confessed how desperate my financial situation had become—and that I didn't see how we could make ends meet. He listened quietly and then said not to worry about paying him back. He never brought it up again—no recriminations, no second-guessing, no "I told you so." He knew I was suffering and had done my best—no need to pile on. At that moment, I was profoundly grateful for that gesture of generosity and grace.

I don't know why expressing himself emotionally to his children was so difficult; it just wasn't part of his chemistry. As in so many families, Mom served as an interpreter. She let me know that Dad was proud of me: she "could just tell." After she died, he made an effort to write supportive letters to us kids regularly, in which he signed off with "love." I appreciated him doing that, and I recognize that it must have been easier to do it in writing than face to face. Still, what's so hard about coming right out and saying, "Son, I love you, and I'm proud of you"? I don't remember him ever doing so. That's why the lyrics of Reba McEntire's song speak to so many people.

> The greatest words I never heard I guess I'll never hear
> The man I thought would never die s'been dead almost a year . . .
> He was good at business, but there was business left to do
> He never said he loved me, guess he thought I knew . . .[2]

Although that song resonates with me, it doesn't define my experience. Maybe, as I would say in my eulogy for Dad, I knew more about how he felt than I thought. I just had to go a little deeper. He may not have said it as directly as men of my generation might say it today, but he obviously communicated a lot about himself to a lot of people. I saw it in his friends, our families, in his relationships, and in the fruits of those relationships. I've seen how his friends responded to a real person, an inner man who was being communicated to them even if not in the modern style. That character was especially shown in his intimate relationships, first with my mother, and then with my stepmother. We were delighted and thankful after the loss of our mother that Dad found someone else with whom to share his life. It's rare enough these days for people to establish one rewarding intimate marriage, much less two. I saw my dad's character in how loved and accepted he became in a new family. I don't know the content of his intimate sharing with his life partners, but I do know the results of those relationships: the loyalty he gave and received, the laughter, the people who enjoyed our family home. They have helped me see the inner man.

That last day at the hospital, I had an intense, powerful, intimate, and spiritual final time together with my dad, and I'm grateful for the privilege of being there—to see how the Holy Spirit worked through my presence, that of my brother and sister, and that of others to bring healing and peace. My dad's final gift to me was to allow me to walk the last way of his journey with him, to be there at the end of his life as he was there at the beginning of mine. Our time together came full circle. It was a "hard blessing," but a blessing nevertheless. Maybe he was saying he loved me enough to trust me with that moment, and he knew I could handle it. Maybe he was saying, "I am proud of you."

"Greetings and peace to you on behalf of the Reese family," I began in my eulogy. "We're glad you're here. I would like to say a few words on behalf of Dad's children, words that I hope will honor him and be a blessing for you. I speak from my own experience, but I hope it speaks for Vance and Eileen too . . . ."

I thanked Dad's friends for their loving support and shared some of the memories and reflections I've expressed above. I think the service would have pleased him. In conclusion, I gave thanks for answered prayer—confident that even in loss and suffering, God had spoken and continues to speak a word of peace and wholeness, of "shalom." In looking for a closing passage, I found one from Lamentations. That particular book of the Bible has a depressing reputation, but in it the writer speaks a word of affirming faith through his sadness: "But this I call to mind, and therefore I have hope: The steadfast love of the Lord never ceases, his mercies never come to an end; they are new every morning; great is thy faithfulness. 'The Lord is my portion,' says my soul, 'therefore I will hope in him'" (Lam 3:21-24).

I suppose I found answers to the questions I started with. Dad loved me and was proud of me in ways that are often difficult for a man to express. God doesn't speak to us directly, either, but that doesn't mean we can't hear God if we pay attention. We experience God's love and unconditional acceptance in many ways, including in the words of our parents, both spoken and unspoken. I was privileged to be able to speak on behalf of the family, and the message was received as I had hoped. Afterward, one of dad's friends approached me with tears in his eyes to request a copy of my remarks to share with his own sons. He said he hoped that one day they would be willing to do for him what I had been able to do for my father. I'm sure a lot of men feel the same way; I know I do. And if we do, Reba's song has a warning for us all about what not to do: "The greatest man I never knew came home late every night / He never had too much to say, too much was on his mind."[3]

Maybe my generation is better about being more open, but I'm sure we still have a way to go. As much as I admired my dad and now better understand his ways, I want to be different. I want to know how to connect the inner and outer man, to be more direct regarding how I feel about my kids, never to have too much on my mind to say I need to say, and to give my sons plenty of material for their own eulogies when the need inevitably comes.

Notes

1. Reba McEntire, "The Greatest Man I Never Knew," from For *My Broken Heart*, MCA Nashville, 1991.

2. Ibid.

3. Ibid.

Chapter 11

A MEMORIAL TO GRACE

When Jacob awoke from his sleep, he thought, "Surely the Lord is in this place, and I was not aware of it." He was afraid and said, "How awesome is this place! This is none other than the house of God; this is the gate of heaven." Early the next morning Jacob took the stone he had placed under his head and set it up as a pillar and poured oil on top of it. He called that place Bethel. (Genesis 28:16-19)

We will use these stones to build a memorial. In the future, your children will ask, "What do these stones mean to you?" Then you can tell them, "They remind us that the Jordan River stopped flowing when the Ark of the Lord's covenant went across." . . . Joshua also built another memorial of twelve stones in the middle of the Jordan. . . . The memorial remains there to this day. (Joshua 4:6-9)

For it is by grace you have been saved, through faith—and this not from yourselves, it is the gift of God—not by works, so that no one can boast. (Ephesians 2:8-9)

As the season often is, Christmas 2005 was a time of reflection on my family—past and present. Each year, I remember all the Christmases past and expect each new one to measure up to the best parts of the earlier ones combined. Of course, no Christmas ever can. I wish somehow that all my family members, past and present, could be together again, could merge into some kind of super-hybrid, seasonal reunion. But I know it's inevitable that families change as we move through time; we gain new members and lose others. And, of course, Christmas leads quickly to New Year's Eve, which always marks for me the anniversary of the unexpected death of my mother. On that last night of 1980, I flew home after hearing of her death, passing through an airport in my private zone of grief with a surreal awareness of revelers all around me, either well under way with their celebration or getting ready for the impending festivities. After that, New Year's lost its appeal for me.

As my clan prepared to gather in 2005 for our usual holiday reunion, someone else was missing. This season was the first after my dad's death. Following his memorial service in May, my brother, sister, and I still had unfinished business. We needed to find a place for his ashes. As I helped plan for that task, I thought about the concept of memorials and how best to complete this one for my dad. I realized it's something we do not only for the one who is memorialized, but also for ourselves and for the ones who will follow and need to remember the love of those who are gone.

Most people in our culture still choose to be buried after they die, and well-recognized tradition dictates that graveside ceremonies follow memorial services. A "final resting place" is clearly established. But custom provides less guidance when the body has been committed to ashes. Where then will the loved one "go," and how, if at all, should one mark the place for the ashes? I'm not sure exactly when our family decided to accept cremation as an alternative to burial, but that's what we chose when my mother died. Although cremation is now more common, I know some of Mom's relatives were traditionalists and questioned my father as to whether it was something she wanted. But he and we felt it was and were comfortable with it. After my mother died, we didn't give much thought as to where she would "go." It all happened so fast. Dad later told us he had simply scattered her ashes on the gravesite of her parents in her hometown.

Before my dad died, we made a point to discuss what he wanted, and he said that place was fine for his ashes too. My brother and sister and I agreed to honor his request the next time we got together. So, shortly after Christmas, we drove with our families to the little town of Shelbyville in Middle Tennessee where my mother grew up. Farmland surrounds this county seat with its courthouse square, known as the home of the Tennessee Walking Horse, an oddity trained to stride with its head upright and legs picked up high with each step, producing a smooth, level gait.

We drove in mini-van procession to the rural farm where my mother lived as a child, over low rolling hills, with dry brown leaves layered under the bare trees of winter. We tried to remember the way. My brother had pieced together directions from the relatives and Google Earth. I strained to picture the "old homeplace," as it was called, a house long since gone— passed out of the family and burned down. In that tin-roofed house, which had that smell of many years of history and living, had stood the four-poster bed with feather mattress that swallowed me up at night as a kid and the iron stoves that burned corncobs for heat. Old-fashioned pictures had hung on the walls.

In the large country kitchen, we ate brown-shelled eggs from the chickens that wandered around the yard, country ham, cornbread, and other good southern cooking (although my grandma used to complain that I "didn't eat enough to feed a bird"). The true nature of the food chain quickly dawned on this city boy when I saw my grandma grab some chickens one morning, wring their necks, and toss them in the trunk of her car so we could take them to sell at the market in town.

I could faintly remember the long country road, Blue Stocking Hollow, that led to the property. The road was bordered by large trees that turned it into a fairy-tale tunnel at night for a little kid arriving after a long drive, peering out from the back seat and struggling to see what lay beyond the headlights. Somewhere nearby was a little pond that I fell into once while trying to fish, turning my vision of the world temporarily green before grown-up hands hauled me back out. There's a black and white photo of me proudly holding the lone fish that pond ever yielded, as I far as I know. We drove by the nearby Pleasant Grove Methodist Church where my mom and dad were married. My grandfather, "W. D.," was one of the leaders of that church and, according to a relative's recollection, always sat near the front facing the pulpit, was often asked to pray, and seemed to her to pray forever. These weren't wealthy farms. They may have had a few hogs and chickens but not a Walking Horse in sight. My mom was the first in her family to go to college (as was my dad in his). When planning to marry my dad, Mom determined that the wedding would have to wait until she had worked at least a year in a teaching job after graduation. She thought she owed it to her parents, who had sacrificed to send her a world away to the big state U.

Closer to town, our family caravan found the cemetery where her mother and father and two brothers are buried. On a cold sunny day, within sight of the building where she went to Central High School, we gathered near the grave marker for my grandparents and prepared to say a few words of remembrance for my dad. That memorial stone, big enough for side-by-side inscriptions to "Walter Dee" and "Adaline E." under the family name "Martin," brought back vivid memories, although I had only been there twice before. A dozen years or so earlier, I had attended a conference at a nearby college and decided to make a pilgrimage to the gravesite. On that day, I had a rough picture in my mind's eye, and the cemetery wasn't large, but I had a hard time finding the marker. My time grew short as I walked up and down the rows, with no one around to ask. I almost gave up. Finally, however, I came upon it and almost immediately began to cry. After the long anticipation of finding that special place, I yielded to the emotional power of the many memories that lived there. I had been in that place only once before as a child, when I attended my first funeral.

My grandfather died two months before I was born, but I could recall being at that place in 1961 at the age of seven when my grandma "Addie" was buried and her name added to the stone. It was the first time I saw grown men cry as I looked around at my uncles, Frank and Orverie. These were the tall men I literally looked up to. In one of my past visits to the family farm, a hog had escaped his enclosure, leading Uncle Frank to pull me onto his shoulders and give hair-raising chase. I didn't know it was possible for a man to run that fast. His feet seemed a long way down as I rode his neck around the field, leaping over gullies, not quite sure what we would do if we actually caught the beast. Seeing my uncles then, their faces stricken with emotion, seemed strange to my young eyes, because except for the funeral event it was a typical family gathering, and those gatherings were always happy times. I knew that my grandma had died; I had seen her the night before in her casket in the funeral home parlor, which in small southern towns is often located in what once was a large, gracious home. I can still recall seeing the marks on her nose where her glasses had sat. But a boy that age doesn't feel the depth of loss that my mother and my uncles felt.

Now, all these years later, I stood near that stone again, this time to say words of observance with our families circled around, and like my uncles before me I felt the emotions coming. I didn't want the kids to expect from my reaction some kind of maudlin, wrenching moment of sadness. Tears have always signified that God is speaking to me, trying to reach me for some reason. Then, they reminded me that we stood on holy ground, and that's basically what I said to honor my dad. My brother, sister, and I took turns pouring his ashes into the hole prepared in the ground, and then all of us—kids and grownups—alternated shoveling the soil back in the hole. Although I was sad and felt the loss of my father, I also felt gratitude standing on that holy ground. Being in a cemetery has a way of reminding me that I am part of a body that began long before I was born and will continue on long after I'm gone. I felt that continuity as my family gathered in memory of families past with infinite possibilities of families future. Looking at the headstone for my grandparents and thinking about my mother and father, I knew I could be there myself—now with my own family—because of their actions, their decisions, and their love.

The fundamental lesson I take from my faith experience is that a gracious God loved us first, before we could do anything to deserve it, and God continues to love us in spite of whatever we may do. Grace doesn't come and go in our lives. The idea of a God who loves us even before birth means we are born into love, immersed in it since before we were old enough to know it. Thinking of my parents and their parents, I see the trans-generational family model of that prior love. Unlike friends, loving though they are, our parents loved us before we were born and before we became the people our friends love now. The Bible dramatizes that kind of love in the many examples of parents who are told in advance of a special child. For the parents of Isaac, John the Baptist, and Jesus, their children became even more significant and special because God's messengers gave them an idea of what they were to become. The parents began to get excited and love those children long before they arrived. Samson's dad, Manoah, was so excited that he pleaded with the angel of the Lord to give him a preview of his promised son: "What is to be the boy's rule of life; what is he to do?" (Judg 13:12).

I felt the accumulated generational love of the "cloud of witnesses" described by the writer of Hebrews (12:1), which was represented by the stones that marked the densely occupied patch of holy ground. In my heart, I felt love for my children and the possibility of children beyond them, which I know my parents and grandparents must have felt for me. Is it any wonder that parents care so much about their children's romantic interests? That's the future; that's *my* future. As much as we may realize that we can't control our children's hearts, the significance of the choice still makes arranged marriages seem appealing! Don't we know our children better than anyone their age? Don't we want and know what will be best for them? Surely they should understand that. But there's only so far we can go to make our hopes for our children a reality. We can hope that the same love we give them will lead them to offer that love to others, and that they will come to expect the same level of respect and intimacy.

I wondered what my grandfather thought as he looked forward in the months before I was born to having a grandchild, his daughter's first child. Was he excited? Did he love my mother? I'm sure he did, and I'm sure she regretted that he died unexpectedly while working in his field a few short weeks before my birth. Grandma suffered the loss of her husband and my mother the loss of her father, but it was time for a new addition to the family and for her to become a parent herself. Perhaps the expectation of a new baby helped with healing, as Grandma came to our home to help my mother. I hope so.

When both parents are gone, we often feel like abandoned little children. Suddenly, we're orphaned. Yet I didn't feel alone standing in the graveyard honoring my father. Yes, our families were together, but even more were with us in spirit. My mother never saw her five grandchildren who stood there that day, but I know she would have loved them and been proud of them. I felt gratitude for the love of those who came before me, which preceded anything I did to deserve it. This makes a parent's love so powerful and the loss of one so profound. As I stood by and reflected on my grandparents' grave marker, it became for me a memorial stone to family grace and to God's grace.

After my dad's death, we had given no real thought to preparing a specific marker stone for him. A strong streak of practicality runs through our family. Who needs a stone? We knew where he was. But family friends said it bothered them that my mom had no permanent marker after she died, no evidence of her existence. Although it seems outdated in the modern era, for genealogists those tombstone rubbings are often the only way to find certain ancestors and information about their lives. Of course, we were there with our children and their children, but I knew what those friends meant. After some reflection, I consulted with my brother and sister, and we agreed that it would be acceptable to prepare a modest gravestone for both our mother and father that would mark the site of their ashes. We would place it flat on the ground atop the graves of my mother's parents.

The Bible recalls many instances of people piling up stones as reminders of significant events. Jacob put a stone in the desert at Bethel after his long night of dreaming. He had encountered God and wanted to memorialize the place and the moment. Joshua piled up stones at the spot of the Jordan River where the Israelites finally entered the promised land. It was an important place, and he wanted to make it special not only for himself but for his children—and their children. Joshua said, "In the future, your children will ask,

'What do these stones mean to you?'" (Josh 6:4, 21). Those who heard him needed to be ready to explain. Nomadic people needed those permanent reminders of the critical events in life, and I suppose we're not much different.

I want my life and my children's lives to serve as memorials too. I wish my parents and grandparents were still here to see them and witness the lives of my family unfold. I wish my mother had lived longer to see my own children. I deeply regret that both my parents didn't live to see their grandchildren. I wish we could have one more Christmas with everyone together again. These are honest longings, and they won't go away. But in God's time they can become part of a larger healing. As I keep piling up the stones in my life's work, I feel the presence of family past. Their love has become an inextricable part of me, and I want to pass it on to my own children. That's a fitting memorial to the infinite grace of God.

IN LOVING MEMORY
Elizabeth Jean Martin Reese
November 3, 1926–December 31, 1980
Donald Reese
March 5, 1924–April 17, 2005

Chapter 12

A SPIRITUAL WALK IN TIME

Now on that same day two of them were going to a village called Emmaus, about seven miles from Jerusalem, and talking with each other about all these things that had happened. While they were talking and discussing, Jesus himself came near and went with them. (Luke 24:13-15)

People these days often describe their spiritual lives as "journeys" or "walks." It may have a certain "new age" sound to it, but I think it's a fitting way to think about faith. Being on a spiritual walk means we're going somewhere important, on a "pilgrimage," and we won't get there all at once. It happens over time. "Seeking a path of faith," as this book's title suggests, leads us to examine the direction of that journey: where we've been, where we are, and where we're going. Finding that path through "everyday life" puts the emphasis on the steps we take each day, requiring a "present-mindedness" that often runs contrary to our nature and the demands of our culture.

Men like me are conditioned to plan, manage, predict, and control. Past performance may not guarantee future results, as the fine print on stock market mutual funds warns, but we hope it comes close. We become fixated on the future, worried about what may or may not happen. In our financial lives, we're encouraged to plan for every possibility and insure against anything that can go wrong. Professional advisers offer us annuities, investments, and long-term care policies to assure our protection and help maintain our current lifestyles in the future. I get the feeling these "experts" would be happiest if I never spent money in the present (and invested it instead with them, of course). After all, I might need it later. I'm supposed to forego the "daily double latte" my whole life so I'll have an extra half-million dollars when I'm seventy. This kind of prediction and planning extends to our professional lives. We want to know where our careers are going and who's going along with us. Becoming aware of God at work in the present moment means giving up the desire for control, and that's tough. Jesus frequently warned his followers not to be anxious about the future, but many of us are paid to be anxious.

Why is it hard to think about the here and now, the daily part of our spiritual walk in time? Even our religious perspectives, which strongly determine how we think about past and future, are distracting. Some people, for example, focus on a salvation moment sometime in the past, separating the time in their lives when they were "unsaved" or "lost" from when they were "saved" and "found." It seems important to them to identify the specific age, place, and moment when they "gave their life to Christ," and that becomes the defining reference point in their spiritual autobiographies. For my evangelical friends in high school and college, the inevitable moment came when they wanted to talk with me alone. They needed to "witness" and find out whether I was a Christian. It never seemed to satisfy them when I said I had been a member of a Christian denomination for years and felt that I had undergone a faith experience. They looked for a specific conversion, "born-again" experience that I could recount (preferably with dramatic flair). As a chronological matter, they posed the fundamental question: where was I now in relation to that pivotal moment—was it yet to come or had it already occurred? It had to be one or the other. For those believers, life was a dualistic separation between pre- and post-salvation periods. If faith requires submission to a higher power, I can understand why it is appealing and simplifying to conceive of that submission as bound within a single moment of being "born again." It dramatically and vividly crystallizes the act of submission and fixes it in time.

Other believers (often in the same theological tradition) dwell on the future in the form of apocalyptic Scripture and the various events said to signal the end times. End-of-the-world movements increased with the coming of the new millennium in 2000, and they are still going strong. That kind of belief proves difficult to shake even when the critical date comes and goes without incident, as in the case of a UFO-believing group from the 1950s documented in the classic study *When Prophecy Fails*.[1] Social psychologist Leon Festinger and his colleagues found that, far from abandoning their beliefs following the "disconfirmation" of a prediction, prophecy followers redoubled their conversion efforts to help soothe their cognitive dissonance. They reinterpreted events to conclude that God had seen their faithfulness and decided to spare the world after all. The defining importance of their end-time belief made it necessary to renegotiate a future date.

When I was in college, Hal Lindsey's book, *The Late Great Planet Earth*, fascinated many people.[2] The end-time speculations based on Revelation, Daniel, and other apocalyptic writers were a staple of many backwoods preachers and televangelists, but also for more upscale evangelical speakers. All kinds of modern signs, including the actions of the then-Soviet Union and the state of Israel, were thought to signal the rise of the anti-Christ, the "second coming," the "rapture," and the thousand-year reign. The chronological sequence of these events—rapture, "tribulation," and millennium—was sometimes in dispute, and I still can't quite keep them straight. Are the believers supposed to be "raptured" away before Jesus returns for his triumphal moment and reign of peace, and, if so, why would they want to miss that? Certain rural churches, in the South especially, are careful to indicate on their front signs their stance on the matter: "pre-millennial." Even in the big city, I've seen the stray bumper sticker that reads, "Warning. In case of rapture, driver will disappear!"

The *Left Behind* series by Tim LaHaye and Jerry Jenkins depict "Earth's last days," and spin-offs include even a video game. The amazing success of this popular culture version of "end times" prophecy cuts across the socioeconomic spectrum and isn't easily dismissed as a backwoods phenomenon. Such perspectives are intensely appealing, especially for those who think they're among the in-group that won't get "left behind." However, the prophets of the Hebrew Bible didn't dwell on the future, unless they warned of the consequences that would ensue if the people remained unfaithful. They urged repentance and strove to reveal how deeply God longed to be in relationship with people, not to predict some Nostradamus-style time line of future events. Why, then, are some so fascinated with "prediction"? Just as we try to manage everything else in our lives, obsessing over future predictions fits our desire to control and reduce anxiety about what lies ahead.

In my personal theology, I have little interest in "end-times" predictions, and I can't restrict the salvation experience to one specific moment in the past. Thinking of my spiritual life as a walk reminds me that God continues to woo me in the present and that saying "yes" to God, surrendering to God, is an ongoing process of submission, rooted in my continuing availability to God's presence.

One of the true personal growth opportunities for me came through a movement called Emmaus, formed around a central experience called the Walk to Emmaus (in the Catholic Church, "Curseo"). This program for spiritual renewal is designed to strengthen the local church by revitalizing disciples and leaders. Emmaus participants come from all walks of life—blue collar, white collar, professionals, and political leaders—with no doctrinal litmus test. With separate events for men and women, the retreat portion of the walk takes place over a long weekend in a carefully constructed and planned schedule, away from the distractions and demands of everyday life and with leadership from both clergy and laypersons. The larger Emmaus community, comprising former participants in the retreat experience, helps conduct the events with music, food, gifts, and prayers. They present talks and provide other practical supports, modeling the servanthood of Christ. After these retreats, many participants continue to gather in small "reunion" groups that meet regularly to give members a chance to discuss the successes and failures in their daily walk.

The Emmaus movement gets its name and central metaphor from a relatively brief incident found only in Luke's Gospel. He tells the powerful and poignant story of Jesus appearing after the crucifixion to two of his followers on the road to Emmaus (Luke 24:13-35). At first, they don't recognize him, but as they talk together Jesus begins to help them understand what happened during the recent days by interpreting the Scriptures.

> As they approached the village to which they were going, he [Jesus] walked ahead as if he were going on. But they urged him strongly, saying, "Stay with us, because it is almost evening and the day is now nearly over." So he went in to stay with them. When he was at the table with them, he took bread, blessed and broke it, and gave it to them. Then their eyes were opened and they recognized him, and he vanished from their sight. They said to each other, "Were not our hearts burning within us while he was talking with us on the road, while he was opening the Scriptures to us?" (Luke 24:28-32)

The two men quickly returned to Jerusalem to meet the other disciples: "Then they told what had happened on the road, and how he had been made known to them in the breaking of the bread" (24:35). Later Jesus appeared again to the disciples and spoke with them, to their joy and amazement. Luke 24:45 recounts, "Then he opened their minds so they could understand the Scriptures."

As I think about this story of a simple but eventful walk, I see a time line of events unfolding. If placed in chronological order, three important moments stand out in the disciples' encounter with Christ: their hearts burned, their eyes were opened, and then their minds were opened, which led them to understand. That's how I understand my faith experience. The grace of God first seeks me on the road and calls me out of myself into relationship. As a result, my heart burns in longing for fellowship with God. When disciples enter into that relationship, symbolized here in the breaking of the bread, eyes are opened, and a new all-encompassing vision for life is revealed. At that point, my mind—which, no matter how I try, cannot reason itself into God's grace—is opened, and I begin to understand.

When Christ helped open these disciples' eyes, he changed their perspective on their own walk in time. Previously, on the road to Emmaus, their present was filled with confusion and emptiness at the absence of their leader. Their past was a source of disappointment and regret, while their future was uncertain and full of anxiety. But then their hearts were warmed, and they pleaded urgently with Jesus, "Stay with us . . . the day is almost over." They seized the present moment, and as a result were able to see Christ. Their present was filled with joy, and they became fully alive. Even in their grief and loss, their past was given new meaning because they could see how it had not merely led them to, but *culminated* in, their present moment. That gave them a future of hope and excitement.

This story reminds me of how easy it is for the "time line" of life to get out of balance. Life at its best is a healthy, present-minded awareness of God that brings the past and future into proper focus. Certain mountaintop moments intensify that awareness, and for many the Walk to Emmaus is one of them—a spiritual "high" that often continues for days afterward. Participants are completely submerged into a structured routine that models the grace of God, being cared for and loved unconditionally by others. That is powerful adrenaline. When men especially are finally given the opportunity to step out of the work world, with all its distinctions of occupation and status, they experience grace and receive permission to express their deepest longings and regrets in a trusting environment (if only to themselves). That is sometimes overwhelming, and for many, including the macho guys, it may be the first time they weep openly in years.

My own Emmaus experience helped open my imagination to how rich the presence of God can be when I am fully immersed in it. God reached me once again and gave me a glimpse of how a faith experience feels. I "experienced" my faith, rather than simply learning more about it. It helped bring together a number of yearnings that were at work in my life. I could better understand David's description in the Psalms of his relationship with God: of "taking delight" in God, of "thirsting" for God's presence, of "hungering" for it, of seeking God's face and being sincerely glad to go to the house of the Lord. In a way that has somehow stuck, I resolved to be more fully open to God's presence in my life and to cultivate that relationship more deeply and intentionally than before.

Many enjoy returning to an Emmaus weekend to work with the team that conducts the event, assisting the new participants ("pilgrims"). In part, it's a way to try to recapture the spiritual "high" that often seems lacking in daily life. Mountaintop experiences are great, but our walk doesn't usually carry us there. Despite my best intentions, the distractions of life set in, and my ability to live on a spiritual level often seems fleeting. I know I'm not the only one who has trouble sustaining my high into the weeks that follow the retreat weekend, when everyone returns to their usual lives where nothing much has changed.[3]

Guys come and go from a reunion group I belong to that meets (with any luck) weekly, saying how important it is to them but honestly acknowledging the difficulty of resisting the pull of busy schedules and other commitments. We find it easy to let the pace of life, the shear banality of our routine, crowd the room that is set aside for our inner lives. Personal spirituality ebbs and flows, but of course that's natural. That's why we need each other, to encourage and help hold each other accountable. I'm more mindful of my faith walk if I know I will discuss it with others, and I begin to make mental notes of things to share. Like everyone, I strive to recapture mountaintop experiences but often feel as if I just go through the motions. That's why I have to remind myself to keep taking those steps, to follow Isaiah's advice: "Seek the Lord while he may be found; call upon Him while he is near" (Isa 55:6). I have to make a conscious daily decision to create routines and spaces where Christ can "stay a while," but, like the disciples, I may have an especially strong sense of God's presence one moment only to feel that he has "vanished" in the next.

Fortunately, even ordinary places can become holy ground. In Luke's account of the walk to Emmaus, we're not sure of the exact place where the disciples asked Jesus to "stay a while." The text simply says they drew near to where they were going. Jesus' presence quickened a desire in them to hold on to him. The disciples were on the way to an unimportant village, to no place in particular. Emmaus is only mentioned this one time in the Bible. We also don't know what the disciples planned to do in Emmaus, but apparently they decided it was unimportant, for they headed immediately back to Jerusalem, the geographical center of their faith. When Christ comes, as he did to those disciples, "no place in particular" becomes transformed, and he becomes known in the breaking of the bread. The men's spiritual encounter changed their direction from no place in particular to someplace special. Fortunately, once our imaginations are open, we receive a vision that is difficult to put away. For me, that vision carries me through periods of ebb and flow and helps me to see God at work in my life—whether in the little things or in the big decisions that confront me.

I've traveled with enough guys to know we like to be aware of the schedule. We want to know what time it is and what time things will happen. If we don't, we get downright agitated, nervous, and pushy. It's hard to give up the need to be on top of the plan, and that also goes for the big picture in life. We all want to know where our lives are heading. Fast-track professionals get on that track by thinking ahead. When we achieve a little success and material comfort, the risks of taking a wrong turn increase. There's more at stake, and for me that drives a desire for greater control, not a faithful surrender. Not long ago, for example, I faced the possibility of a major job change. Colleagues at another university encouraged me to consider a leadership position there, a move that would have involved a huge shift for my family and me: in community, in type of job, in everything. In many ways it seemed like an excellent fit for someone with my background and abilities, and it's always flattering to receive such an invitation.

At first, I didn't want to consider the possibility; I was comfortable. In the past, when given other such opportunities, I agonized over the decisions, recognizing how much rode on them. Absorbed for weeks and even months with the matter, I would labor over analyzing the pros and cons, wearing my poker face until finally I rehearsed the phone call, the one in which I would politely decline the offer. I get nervous about the prospect of leaving my colleagues and friends, a city I'm deeply familiar with, and the church community that feeds me spiritually. I've learned my way around well after all these years: I know how to find the post office, the bank, and an honest mechanic. But I wonder if that comfort level may limit how I allow God to guide me. If I'm honest with myself, I might also admit that I am fearful of extending myself into a position that may not suit me and might be difficult to reverse, of the possibility of failure in a high-profile role that would make failure more obvious. Of course, any decision of mine affects my family too, and that's a big responsibility. The prospect of moving was easier when I was younger, before I acquired so much stuff, when I didn't have so much to lose. In moving out of my last bachelor apartment, I was pressed for time. Having already packed and shipped my books, I jammed the rest of my stuff into a few Hefty trash bags and threw them in the back of the car. I was delighted just to have a job to go to and leave graduate school and student life behind.

Mid-career opportunities, however, arouse other concerns, and I was moved to pray and seek guidance about this one. Moving would definitely take a lot longer now, so I hoped for clear instructions. I thought about the familiar verses in which God—following the death of Moses—tells a no doubt nervous Joshua three times to be "courageous": "Do not be frightened or dismayed, for the Lord your God is with you wherever you go" (Josh 1:9). A similar spirit is expressed in Psalm 37: "Commit your way to the Lord; trust in him, and he will act" (v. 5). Of course, God may not act right away to tell me what to do, but I am supposed to "Be still before the Lord, and wait patiently for him" (Ps 37:7). I am called to have faith that God will lead me where he wants me to be. I'm usually suspicious of mass-market inspirational bestsellers like *The Prayer of Jabez*, with its basic message that it's okay for us to ask for God's blessing, that God is waiting to bless us. Nevertheless, I found in it a more intriguing idea: "We are expected to attempt something large enough that failure is guaranteed . . . unless God steps in."[4] I'm not interested in the possibility of failure. For a liberal, I have grown much more conservative when it comes to my career. At the time this job suggestion came to me, I wondered if perhaps I was afraid to think big.

We usually think of fear as a reaction to something bad, but of course it's just as possible to be afraid of the unknown, of giving up something good, even if God may want us to have something better. I know what I have now, and the status quo looks good; I'm not sure what lies in store if I step beyond it. But, as Paul says, "God did not give us a spirit of timidity, but a spirit of power . . ." (2 Tim 1:7), and this spirit comes about by being present-minded, open, and alive to God's direction. I found myself wishing that God would just go ahead and tell me what to do next. Well, God already had, saying in Proverbs, "Trust in the Lord with all your heart; lean not to your own understanding, but in all your ways acknowledge him and He will make straight your path" (3:5-6). This passage helped. When I began to think this way and pray that God would strengthen my spirit of trust, suddenly it became all right to consider a big change, and I felt more relaxed about it.

Without knowing the professional outcome, I trusted that God would lead my family and me to the right decision. In the end, the job offer never came, but there will probably be others. Whatever the outcome, I'll have to do the same kind of work, to trust and be confident that I'll find the right place for me. God wants my present before he's able to give me a future.

Emotions of faith are deeply rooted in time. When our eyes are closed to the presence of God in the present, our walk becomes like the walk of those two men on the road to Emmaus. We hold to a past that drags us down and burdens us with remorse and regret, and we foresee a future filled with fear and anxiety. Living in that kind of past and dwelling on that kind of future hollows out the present, leaving little room for the joy of being fully alive. The past is a source of thanksgiving when we see how it culminated—through the good and bad—in our present moment, where God is always faithful. When a "third" joins us on our walk, we become alive to God in our present and our hearts burn within us. Then the rest of our journey—where we've been and where we're going—makes sense. Each step we take leads us into an uncertain future, but we can only hope that those are steps of faith. A loving God—who is with us right now, at this time, in this place—helps us celebrate our past with gratitude and anticipate our future with hope.

Notes

1. Leon Festinger, Henry W. Riecken, and Stanley Schachter, *When Prophecy Fails* (Minneapolis: University of Minnesota Press, 1956).

2. Hal Lindsey, with C. C. Carlson, *The Late Great Planet Earth* (Grand Rapids: Zondervan, 1970).

3. More information about the Emmaus community may be found at http://www.upperroom.org/emmaus/.

4. Bruce Wilkinson, *The Prayer of Jabez: Breaking Through to the Blessed Life* (Sisters OR: Multnomah, 2000) 20.

Chapter 13

COMPETITIVE FAITH

*I press on toward the goal to win the prize for which God has called me heaven-
ward in Christ Jesus. (Philippians 3:14)*

As I get older, I miss the mentors and encouragers I had as a young man, the
father figures who were there for me. Many of them are gone now, including
my dad. I know it's the natural way of things that I play that role now, but
I'm nostalgic for the time when I was the one being mentored. I was good at
that, at taking advice, at being encouraged, and I'm not so sure I'm good at
doing it for others. After all, I'm too young to be a father figure. I suppose
we never outgrow the need for a good coach. We need people who can point
out what we can't see, to do for us what we can't do for ourselves, to help us
set goals, to hold up an image for us to grow into. When we seek that kind of
help, we honor the importance of whatever work we do, and we say that it
deserves a better effort. Fortune 500 executives have "career coaches," and it
seems natural that professional musicians return to their teachers for tune-
ups. The golfer whose swing isn't working anymore needs that kind of help,
and of course most athletes work with coaches intensively throughout their
playing years. No one considers such mentoring a sign of weakness. The
stakes are too high for these people to ignore help.

There's a faith lesson in this. If guys can learn from anything, it ought to
be sports. We're hard-wired to be fans, maybe because we need to find organized way to channel our emotions. I often think it gives us something
convenient to talk about so we don't have to get too personal. Sports are a
common foundation for small talk that doesn't have to lead anywhere—certainly nowhere intimate. The irony of sports is that it allows us to care

passionately about something that doesn't mean anything. Beyond their function as a social lubricant and underneath the layers of polite society, the rougher contact sports connect us to something primal in our personalities. As boys, physical strength marked our status, and the occasional fistfight (which I did my best to avoid) helped confirm the order of things, even into the high school years. For adults, individual combat is frowned on, so we have to find other ways to keep score. That includes identifying with sports teams, our vicarious participation in a larger struggle. In many fan cultures around the world, hooligan spectators still do their own fighting; English soccer fans are particularly good at it. But most of us consider athletes our proxy warriors who fight on our behalf. In a world where the rules for success are often unclear and uncertain, sports give us at least one island of unambiguous structure where we can play out our competitive instincts.

It's not just the men. In many communities, Friday nightlife centers on high school football, the athletes on the field, their cheerleaders and fans, the younger kids milling around in the end zone in constant Brownian motion. As in many southern schools, in mine the football jocks topped the social hierarchy. They represented everyone else as a focus for school identity and "pride." I felt sure too that they had the best shot at scoring with the cheerleaders, who held similar status. One of my best friends was on the team, certifying his place in the pecking order and getting him voted "most popular" for the yearbook. I knew I could never get into real trouble with him around.

By the college years, athletes become more remote and no longer part of the campus social hierarchy. Their lives are set apart, at least in the big-time programs, and have little to do with the lives of other students. The experience for fans also gets more remote as it grows more spectacular and the stadiums more gigantic, with the overpaid coaching the undereducated. That distant spectacle is a cautionary lesson for the Christian life. We are tempted to be religious spectators and rely on others to uphold our "pride," to be passive observers and stay distracted from what really matters. The wrong kind of competition defines our identity. We feel good when we win and depressed when we lose, or at least when our team loses.

I suspect that kind of "team" mentality has given religion a bad name over the years. People have done nasty things to other human beings, claiming they did them for "God" when they were actually trying to get wins for the team at the expense of the other side. God is hard to understand, which I suppose is the point of God, but that creates a problem for us because we don't like too much mystery, so we're always trying to put God into concepts that are easier to handle. We want rules, to know which team we belong to, to have a way to keep score, and to know when we've won.

I enjoy watching sports as much as the next guy. It's a bond of experience that connects me to something difficult to describe, some sense of community, some feeling that I am part of something bigger than myself. In that respect, sports sounds like a religious experience, and I suppose for many it is. When it comes to fan loyalty, we get fixed on whatever we grew up with. As long as I've lived in Texas, I'm still a Tennessee Volunteer fan at heart. Watching their games often gives me a pang of homesickness, not for a place but for something I can't go back to anymore—the place where my encouragers once lived, the town I wasn't fond of until I had to leave it. Now none of the family, the home part of the place, remains there. Those football helmets still look the same, however, with the big orange "T" that hasn't changed in all these years. The Vols connect me to something important in my childhood and remind me of how much my team's success mattered to me then. As a kid, I avidly relived Saturday's football game while reading the Sunday paper.

I can picture General Bob Neyland, the legendary coach for whom the stadium is named, captured in a photograph standing on the sidelines in a long brown winter coat, the kind coaches don't wear anymore, his hand on the shoulder of a player who kneels beside him, waiting for the word to go into the game. Neyland had a mystical look. How do we remember such things so clearly years later? Even today, when watching a tight game, I have to stand up on a critical play, or better yet, turn off the television (the team seems to do better when I'm not watching). I can vividly recall anticipating the Orange Bowl game on New Year's Day 1968, when Tennessee prepared to play the Oklahoma Sooners. The Vols had a great team that year, and I desperately wanted them to win. My dad (a passive fan at best) and I watched the big event in the den at home, and as the game took a turn for the worse, he began to find it funny. Maybe that was his way of coping, but I was wounded and demanded to know how he could laugh at a time like that. Tennessee narrowly lost, and I was dejected for days. Why did I care so much about the outcome? Because part of my identity was wrapped up in the team. The fact that I wasn't any better or worse off as a result of the outcome didn't matter; serious fans know what I mean. That's a harmless example, but remembering the way I felt reminds me of the dark side of competition in other parts of our lives. An important part of ourselves can get completely wrapped up in something that doesn't much matter. We get carried away to the point that the goal becomes to win, not to master the skills that lead to winning.

Even the language of competition distorts our thinking when it is corrupted and finds its way into areas where it doesn't belong. Athletes become "warriors" going into battle. An Alabama coach, following an unexpected loss, foolishly compared it to catastrophic events like 9/11 and Pearl Harbor. More troubling is when military action is described with sports metaphors. Americans like to win, so presidents and their generals claim that a certain policy will lead to a "win." But what will we win? In my academic life, I've often thought about how the media leads the public to understand and respond to war, and I'm disturbed at how easily we reduce military conflict to a game. Around the time of the 1991 Persian Gulf War, "Desert Storm," American supporters of the administration's decisions gathered on several occasions (including on my campus) to chant "USA, USA!" as though it were a Super Bowl. In more recent years, who knows what "winning" the so-called war on terrorism would look like? Unlike in war, which has larger objectives for power and control of territory, the goal in sports is simply to win the game. The winners may receive a big trophy, but they don't get to pillage and sack the enemy's lands and carry off the women and children and make them slaves. War as sports is not a good analogy. It oversimplifies something we prefer not to think more deeply about, much as we often prefer to avoid thinking too seriously and too critically about our faith.

The language of sports leads us to think about who's on our team—whether Team America or Team Jesus. You are for us or against us. At the state capitol recently, a Texas legislator walked out on the prayer of a Muslim Imam, saying he didn't want to imply with his presence that he endorsed the message. Unfortunately, many others like him fear that someone else's religious observance will diminish their own. My local paper carried a story of an evangelical mega-church turning down a request to use one of its facilities for an annual inter-religious worship service when it learned that non-Christians would participate. That's the negative side of competition, when we become too focused on who's on the team and think of spirituality as a zero-sum game. I can't believe God wants us to think of it that way.

We all compete for something, of course, and that's not necessarily bad. It's the way we measure how we stack up, how we're doing. The positive face of competition includes hard work, selflessness, loyalty, concentration on a goal, and self-sacrifice. We need to be passionate and disciplined about a goal, challenging ourselves to go beyond our current limits. Team members must work together for the good of the group. The longer we stay out of shape, the harder it is to get back in shape. Athletes don't decide one day that they're ready to compete; it's a lifestyle. They train and become consistent with the fundamental techniques of their sport. They have to practice. They can't turn their skills on and off. These also are lessons for the spiritual life.

When technique becomes instinct, the athlete enters a zone of pure performance where technique disappears—a sense of flow where one is no longer conscious of the passage of time but simply revels in the joy of the moment. The practices and techniques of religion are meant to help us get closer to God, and when they work right, we find ourselves in a place of pure worship where time and space fall away. It's like the kind of spiritual "flow" Moses urged for the Israelites in Deuteronomy: "These are not mere words, these are your life" (Deut 32:47). I hear him saying that these are not empty techniques; rather, we should enter them completely, trusting them to lead somewhere. To the extent people have a positive image of religion, I think they have this kind of competition in mind, the kind of drive that religion encourages within us to be more disciplined, to serve, and to love.

Our culture gives successful coaches a lot of credibility. Their books and leadership courses promise to teach the secrets of success in life. An informal poll at the bookstores suggests that the basketball coaches are ahead in this regard. I suppose they tend to get closer to their players. The teams are smaller, and they can get more directly involved in coaching the whole person. Football coaches always seem more distant with extra layers of staff between them and the players. (And they always wear those headphones.) The best ones have a healthy perspective on competition, and their players remember them for teaching more than the game. These coaches teach about being a man. Dean Smith of North Carolina was like that. His players revered him for showing them about how to live beyond the basketball court.

Bobby Knight was a successful coach, and many of his players were loyal to him, but I don't think he found joy in competition. His players endured constant negativity and criticism, and it worked to some extent, but it seems like a poor model. Steve Alford, one of Knight's star players, said Knight grew angry when players didn't want something for themselves as much as he wanted it for them. The great sports book, *Season on the Brink* by John Feinstein, tracks the championship year of Knight's Indiana basketball team and offers an insider view.[1] By the end of the account, however, I was left with an oppressive feeling from the tension and anxiety of playing under Knight—and the awful darkness that followed defeats.

I get a much different sense from reading about UCLA's John Wooden. He didn't talk much about winning, although he won more titles than anybody else probably ever will. UCLA star Bill Walton said, "John Wooden was hired to teach basketball at UCLA, but he taught life. Always positive, always constructive." Walton recalls that practices were structured around the four laws of education: explanation, demonstration, correction, repetition. Wooden had a widely quoted definition of success: "Success is peace of mind, which is a direct result of self-satisfaction in knowing you made the effort to do the best of which you are capable."

The Apostle Paul illustrated both sides of competition in his life. Paul was undoubtedly a competitive guy. He had that kind of personality and drive, but he changed in mid-life from the dark side of competition to the positive side. Before his Damascus Road experience, he competed to see who could be the most observant Jew, a Hebrew born of Hebrews from the tribe of Benjamin, a Pharisee, and, according to the law, blameless. He persecuted those who weren't on the same team before coming to a much more expansive idea of who the team really was. After that, the dividing lines fell away: "There is one body and one Spirit—just as you were called to one hope when you were called—one Lord, one faith, one baptism; one God and Father of all, who is over all and through all and in all" (Eph 4:4-6).

Paul still had a keen sense of the power of team mentality when he defended himself before the Roman tribune. Acts tells the story of how Paul realized that there were Sadducees and Pharisees among the onlookers whom Paul knew differed on the idea of the resurrection of the dead. He was able to derail the meeting by claiming he was on trial for that belief, sending the two factions into violent arguing with each other (Acts 23). By that time in his life, he recognized the emptiness of that kind of competition, counting it as "rubbish" and loss compared to knowing Christ (Phil 3). At the end of his life, Paul had peace of mind knowing he had done his best: "I have *fought* the good *fight*, I have finished the *race*, I have kept the faith" (2 Tim 4:7, my emphasis).

Remember John Wooden's saying about success being a peace of mind knowing you did your best? That sounds like Paul, whose letters are full of sports images, especially in Philippians: "I press on toward the goal to win the prize for which God has called me heavenward in Christ Jesus" (Phil 3:14). Paul knew that if he were to keep growing in his life, he needed a big goal. In his competitive zeal, he wanted to win the most worthwhile thing imaginable: he wanted to win Christ, to know Christ, to know the surpassing power of his resurrection. When Paul talks about running the good race, whom do you think he raced against? Only himself, toward what he hoped to be in Christ.

Paul was a great coach in his work with the early churches. Like John Wooden with his players, Paul wanted something for his struggling Christian churches as much or more than he wanted it for himself. He didn't ask anything of them that he didn't ask of himself. He loved them so much it hurt, and he was constantly in the process of teaching, encouraging, correcting, and teaching some more—all in love. Like Bill Walton said, Paul believed in "explanation, demonstration, correction, repetition." He gave his hearers a positive vision of life in Christ, lifting them out of their past lives, their own worst tendencies and instincts.

> Finally, brothers, whatever is true, whatever is noble, whatever is right, whatever is pure, whatever is lovely, whatever is admirable—if anything is excellent or praiseworthy—think about such things. Whatever you have learned or received or heard from me, or seen in me—put it into practice. (Phil 4:8-9)

That's basic sports psychology—visualize success. Paul warned the Colossians to set their minds on "things that are above" and built their confidence (Col 3:1-2). In one of the most encouraging and inspiring prayers in the Bible, Paul gave the Ephesians a tremendous message:

> For this reason I kneel before the Father . . . . I pray that out of his glorious riches he may strengthen you with power through his Spirit in your inner being, so that Christ may dwell in your hearts through faith. And I pray that you, being rooted and established in love, may have power, together with all the saints, to grasp how wide and long and high and deep is the love of Christ, and to know this love that surpasses knowledge—that you may be filled to the measure of all the fullness of God. (Eph 3:14)

Paul knew there could be no competition among children of God because we are one body, with one Lord, one cup of blessing that we share. There is only the competition within ourselves to be more of what the grace of God calls us to be.

Note

1. John Feinstein, Season on the Brink (New York: Macmillan, 1986).

Chapter 14

TALKING ABOUT GOD

Therefore go and make disciples of all nations, baptizing them in the name of the Father and of the Son and of the Holy Spirit, and teaching them to obey everything I have commanded you. (Matthew 28:16-20)

Whoever publicly acknowledges me I will also acknowledge before my Father in heaven. But whoever publicly disowns me I will disown before my Father in heaven. (Matthew 10:32-33, TNIV)

In the "great commission," Jesus commanded his followers to make disciples of all nations. I confess I've always been uncomfortable with that instruction. As interpreted by some believers, the commission seems like a kind of spiritual "pyramid scheme" in which one's status in the organization is tied to the number of new recruits (souls) won for Christ. We are, it seems, to go public with the message, and elsewhere in the Gospels Jesus builds in accountability moments for good measure: whoever acknowledges Jesus, he'll acknowledge before God ("And whoever publicly disowns me . . . "). I always worried about those passages. The born-agains used them as a stick to make the conversion moment more urgent. I remember going to a movie theater for a film in junior high that was sponsored by an evangelical group. The free admission should have tipped me off. After the movie, they held an "altar call," and, using the quote from Matthew above about acknowledging Christ, they invited kids to come up on stage (I didn't go). I had a picture in my formative years of Jesus going through a lineup at the final reckoning, consulting his notes and picking out the ones who went public about him while they had the chance. "Acknowledge," "confess" in other translations—

they amounted to the same thing. I stand up for Jesus, and he stands up for me when it really counts, when it's time for the meeting with "the Big Guy."

I agree it seemed like a fair proposition, but somehow it was never my style. Couldn't there be an accommodation for people like me: a Christian but not a "*Christian*"? What if I don't feel comfortable being a stand-up guy for Jesus? I always feel embarrassed for those athletes and celebrities who seem compelled to confess the mantra that Jesus is Lord of their lives. Yes, that's great, now let's move on. It's bad form.

The Mormons and Jehovah's Witnesses do the extreme witnessing. I have to admit that they put themselves on the line for their beliefs. They seem agreeable enough, but when I see them in the neighborhood I pretend I'm not home. Catholics evangelized much of the world with tough love conversion in some cases. That seemed to wear them out, and they don't go door to door anymore. I knew an older gentleman while I was in college, an Italian guy and a huge opera fan. We got together every now and then to listen to music. Once after I'd known him for a while, I asked out of curiosity, "Dick, what religion are you?" He looked puzzled and said, "I'm Catholic, of course," (as in "What are you, some kind of idiot? I'm Italian."). The religion simply went with the territory, and you need not do any recruiting for the team. They already had plenty of members.

The Jews have it easy that way. They are born Jewish, except for the dedicated converts, and the Jews make those come to them and work at it. (Even then I'm not sure they have full "chosen people" membership.) At the Billy Graham Crusade you could take care of the whole business in less than ten minutes. It's the Protestants who seem to have been given the job of sales force for Christianity, and the evangelicals have lowered the transaction time to a minimum. Bow your head, say a simple prayer, and you're in. I always hated selling stuff; people would always pretend they weren't home.

Why am I not more eager to talk about God out in public, away from the safe zone of church and other "God places"? Why shouldn't I be ready to give my Jesus story? Because it is something precious and intimate that I don't take casually. I like to think it through before speaking up and trying to convince someone else to buy it, which is probably why I prefer to write it down. What about the message I send and the witnessing I do with my life without actually talking about it? Doesn't my behavior in my everyday life give a testimony? That always seemed like a good compromise: I live a good life and don't have to do any direct sales. But is that what Jesus meant by "acknowledge"? Maybe I'm a reluctant witness, but it's hard for me to sum up my response to God with the code words that "I've given my life to Christ" (even if I have). I am drawn to God through my Christian experience, I approach and experience God through Christ. The life of Jesus is central to that experience, but Jesus, as a man and as a name, is not the same as my faith. Saying I submit to Jesus seems to sell Jesus short. Christ is bigger than Jesus.

One way or the other, without planning it, I find that religion has crept into my public life, the me that's out "in the world," including the part of the world where I work. In my head, I think about my professional life as part of my faith and use my faith experience to make sense of my work. But that's different from thinking about it as a subject, as content, as something I will actually talk about—something to which I actually admit. When it comes to the classroom, I know that any mention of religion has to be done carefully and with judgment, but in a few instances I have revealed some aspects of my faith experience that in years past I would have kept to myself. When Jesus says I must "acknowledge" him, I suppose that means at least to be honest about who I am as a person, to be open about having a faith identity and to find a way to do it while still being "professional."

To understand how faith and teaching mix, I have to explain about how it works in the classroom. I teach a large introductory course about journalism, mainly for freshmen and sophomores. We deal with controversial issues that are in ready supply, especially when it comes to the news and politics during an election season. One week, a student wrote me a note wondering whether I should try to be more objective. That was a good question: should I be? After all, the subject was journalism, which is built on objectivity (or at least the idea of it). The objectivity question rarely comes up in chemistry or geology, where the instructor's political or religious views are irrelevant. But fields in the humanities and social sciences—including journalism—are more naturally related to politics and points of view.

Conservative students on my campus and others keep "watch lists" of faculty whom they think push a political agenda. They even go to the point of sitting in on classes, reviewing syllabi, and checking reading materials (something it's often difficult to get faculty to take the time to do when evaluating their colleagues). Other groups across the country are convinced that left-leaning professors are brainwashing their classes and penalizing anyone who strays from liberal orthodoxy. I see no evidence of that, but it hasn't stopped one conservative activist from putting two of my colleagues on his book's "most dangerous professors" list. I don't think I'm on the verge of being "dangerous" yet, but I think I'd prefer it to being boring. Unfortunately, students often don't appreciate—and regard as biased—anything that contradicts what they already believe. Even in a university community, the fundamentalist impulse can work against learning and growth. I definitely take my responsibility seriously when teaching a large class, particularly when it's required for our majors. They deserve to have the material presented fairly, and they don't have the luxury of shopping around for a more simpatico instructor who fits their political leanings.

Thus, we have to be careful about defining the issues and showing how evidence supports positions. There may be occasional "advocates" who in extreme (and rare) cases bully their positions even when they are irrelevant to the subject. That's an offense to good teaching, of course. Students need to be taught to think for themselves and be open to other points of view, and each teacher must select the best ways to accomplish that. The "sphinxes" pride themselves on their ability to hide personal positions. Students want to please and conform to what they perceive to be the "right position," so a strong point of view from a professor often derails discussion and inhibits students finding their own conclusions. The "balancers" admit to a point of view but claim they expose students to a wide array of positions nonetheless. If not handled properly, the "on-one-hand vs. the-other-hand" approach can become dull and disingenuous if the instructor clearly thinks there is weak evidence for one of the "hands." Students are sensitive to any hint of "bias" if the "balance" shifts too far in one direction. Like some of their parents, they think anything they don't already agree with is biased by definition.

Finally, what I might call an "engaged analyst" admits to a point of view (or a broader scholarly approach) and attempts to reveal how he or she arrived at it. To that person, it is a way of seeing the world and the evidence, not merely a partisan opinion with another "side" left out. I mix it up among these styles but find myself using this approach more often. "Objectivity" suggests a detachment, a disinterested approach, but good teaching needs engagement. On some issues, I can't pretend that, after all these years of thinking and reading, I have not developed a thoughtful position. But presenting it requires a certain personal transparency so others can see why I think the way I do. That sometimes means getting more personal, and getting more personal may lead to moments when I can actually acknowledge my faith experience. Teaching (and I suppose discipleship) involves not only covering the material but also modeling a way of approaching the world.

Of course, when it comes to religion, I believe classroom watchdogs are more concerned with professors suppressing or ridiculing beliefs (remember, we're all secular humanists) than expressing their own. When would it be appropriate for me to mention my faith experience? The answer is only when it's appropriate to the objective and then very carefully. For example, I once gave a lecture about religion and journalism to help show how important it is for journalists to cover that subject better. Many stories now have a religious dimension, including the rising political influence of the Religious Right, and issues of faith are unavoidable. Because students often assume that journalists are anti-religion, I provide evidence that they are not. They simply don't like complicated or "sensitive" stories, and religion is both. The elite media, and the people who work for them, aren't located in the South where most evangelical Christians live. They lack familiarity with each other.

Because of the demographics, many journalists haven't related as well as they might to the faith community. They have jumped to conclusions about "moral issues" voters and about the "Christian" position on public policies, limiting faith issues to abortion and gay marriage. Because students may also assume that professors, and therefore I, may be antagonistic toward religion, I let them know otherwise. During my lecture, I said President Bush and I had once attended the same Methodist church, and that although we part ways politically (way apart), I suspected I shared more in my faith experience with him than I did with his challenger, the Catholic John Kerry. I didn't make that admission gratuitously, but I think it served a purpose. Critical thinking means avoiding a jump to the conclusion that being Christian automatically equals something politically. If only for a passing moment, it's good to undermine some of the stereotypes about who gets to claim the label "person of faith." I do. Maybe they can too.

Faith is closely tied to matters of personal conscience, and this often comes up when discussing professional issues. It should, considering the many ethical scandals in the professions. How should professionals act, and how should personal conscience guide them? We talked one day in class about a television reporter in Memphis. I showed a story he did about the city's mayor fathering a child out of wedlock with a woman who had decided to reveal it on camera. Why did she decide to give this reporter an exclusive? Because, as the reporter revealed in the story, they both shared a belief in Jesus Christ. God had arranged the meeting, he said, compelling him to "give God the glory." He "simply obeyed God," regardless of whatever persecution might come. To me, the "testimony" seemed jarring and out of place.

It came where it wasn't expected, in the middle of a routine story about a political scandal.

I left the issue open for the students as to how sincerely motivated they thought the reporter was, but to me nothing about his handling of the story glorified God. The reporter claimed he was boldly sharing his faith, as he was taught, but that sounded contrived. It rang false, even if he didn't intend it that way. Part of me might once have felt a grudging respect for the guy. Once I may have thought he was being courageous; now I think he's a self-promoter. He used the faith angle as a hook to get an interview ahead of the competition, to get a story, and to promote himself, pandering to a largely conservative Christian audience and rationalizing it as an act of courage. I took a "sphinx" approach in that discussion, but in bringing it up, I hoped to suggest that just because someone says he's motivated by faith and says the magic Jesus words doesn't mean he made the right choice. Confessing Christ means more than that.

The younger students are impressionable. They're searching for their religious identity, and many of them are having their old one threatened. But the older ones, the doctoral students, are looking for their own direction in life. They often get into an existential funk about whether they've made the right choice, whether they will ever have a great idea and find a job in the career in which they've invested so much. I worked with such a group a few years ago, and I included a discussion about their "mission in life." Again, I've become more personal in teaching during the last several years, and the vision thing seems to go along with that. Early on, much of the "voice" in my lectures belonged to my own teachers, but has been steadily replaced with my own. As I grow, I think it's natural to progress from teaching what I've been taught to teaching what I've lived. I encouraged my students to spend time on their personal direction so we could talk about it. All those self-help books seem silly when they suggest sitting down and writing a mission statement, but it's harder than it looks. There's something about writing these things down, putting them into words, that makes you wonder if that's really what you want to say. I figured I should be prepared to do one of my own, and I shared the one below with my students. I said that for me, I found it important to organize my life around a spiritual dimension and work from there.

> I seek to keep my life centered upon my spiritual relationship with God. Each day I seek to grow in my discipleship by investing time and energy in my faith journey. I seek to live intentionally, consciously and actively seeking to order

my activities around goals and behave according to my beliefs, defining for myself my life's work.

That was the faith part, nothing more than that, but I included it with some trepidation. Some were surprised but grateful for my opening that kind of subject. Were we allowed to talk about that? We didn't talk about it much, but it was significant for me to talk about it at all. It seemed like a simple thing; I simply had never done it before. I wasn't advocating or telling them what to believe. I just said what I found to be important for myself, and I believe they were mature enough to hear it.

The rest of my professional mission would not come as much of a surprise. Now, reading it again after a few years, my words sound grandiose, but I expressed as best I could what I'm trying to do and how I want to do it. It also sounds daunting, but that may be the point.

My integrity means my public and private selves must be in honest agreement with each other and organized around my basic beliefs. I have been richly blessed with talents and opportunities to learn and freely decide how I direct my energies. I am dedicated to using these gifts wisely to accomplish worthy goals to provide leadership in service. I will resist dwelling on the limits that constrain me, focusing instead on the opportunities all around me.

I will discipline my use of time, devoting it wisely to my priorities, which I will be constantly evaluating. I cherish the autonomy and independence of academic life and regard membership in a university community as a privilege. I will strive to uphold the best values of the intellectual life, avoiding cynicism and resignation to the status quo.

I will communicate honestly but supportively with my colleagues, helping and encouraging them to do their best work. I will strive to connect more deeply with the lives of students, treating each of them with respect.

Through my teaching I seek to develop the potential of each student, encouraging them to be active thinkers and appreciate the joy of learning.

In my research, I aspire to intellectual courage, saying those things I truly believe in, avoiding being co-opted by other interests than my own personal convictions.

In my service leadership, I try to create a vision and environment, which allows everyone to grow and do their best work. Given the demands of my job, I will strive to guard and strengthen my emotional stamina, practicing an optimistic imperturbability that makes it more difficult for the vision to be undermined.

Maybe I've moved a little further along in my willingness to "testify." The commandment says I'm supposed to love the Lord with all my heart and soul and might, and that means it's hard to keep life compartmentalized. God pulls on me no matter where I am. I keep saying, "God, I've got a firewall going here. I'm out in public; this is not where I let that part of me out. Wait until I get with my other God friends; no one here knows I'm like that." Whatever happened to "Don't ask, don't tell?" I don't want people to cringe when they hear my Jesus story. "Damn, what happened to him?" I want them to think it sounds honest, something that's been thought through and that sounds a little like them, and maybe something they've wondered about. I have to talk about what works for me. Who is Christ for me? I am willing to acknowledge that, and even to dig out some of the connections between my faith experience and the rest of my life and lay them out there. There are ways to be a whole person and do it authentically.

I mentioned that I'm the kind of guy who likes to think things through, to write them down. I've done plenty of writing in my work, but this is different. This is about life, and that's more important, and that makes it harder. The irony is that these issues of faith, for which I've received no formal training and claim no special expertise, may be the kind of writing that resonates with others the most and has more of an impact than any of my other work. Faith is life, and everyone is interested in life. I'm still working on that part, and I'm still not much of a salesman—but I'm willing to testify to my effort.

Chapter 15

HEALTH FOR THE JOURNEY

My back is filled with searing pain; there is no health in my body. (Psalm 38:7)

Why are you downcast, O my soul? Why so disturbed within me? Put your hope in God, for I will yet praise him, my Savior and my God. (Psalm 42:11)

If I rise on the wings of the dawn, if I settle on the far side of the sea, even there your hand will guide me, your right hand will hold me fast. (Psalm 139:9-10, 23)

Along the spiritual journey are many places where we are invited to do the "letting go" work that the Franciscan priest Richard Rohr says is the basis of all spirituality.[1] These moments of dislocation and disorientation involve experiences that lift us out of the "business as usual" flow of events that make up everyday life. For most of us, one such moment of dislocation inevitably arrives in the form of a health crisis. When I suffer through one—removed from usual self, the healthy self of well-being—I am challenged to do that kind of letting go work as I journey from wellness to illness and hopefully back again.

There's nothing like an illness to make me feel vulnerable, to jeopardize my sense of well-being. As a younger man, I didn't think much about health, but like other baby boomers my age, increasingly I must. We start life with the lone pediatrician, later replaced on our personal medical team by a growing group of specialists for every body part. Always the great leveler, illness strips away the protections we thought we had, and such vulnerability doesn't feel good. We fear it. The weakness of our bodies brings a heightened sense of neediness and desire for God at its most basic level, a hope that God will cure us and protect us from future ailments. Don't most prayer requests relate to a health problem? We wish God would rescue us from what illness and injury actually mean—involuntary vulnerability, a threat to our existence, and a reminder of our mortality. We want to move quickly past suffering and get back to our old selves; however, the journey leads not around but *through* suffering.

In his description of his illness, writer and teacher Parker Palmer recounts his experience with clinical depression, which he describes as a great hand crushing him down. In time, however, a therapist gave him an image that led to healing: rather than an oppressive force, he envisioned the hand of a friend pressing him down to the ground where it was safe. From his previous ungrounded life of inflated, high-flying ego, Palmer writes of how he came to view illness as pressing him "inward" and "downward," toward the hard realities of life but also toward grace, healing, and community.[2] I would like to believe that's the way it works, but it's difficult when I'm in the middle of my own experience, even if I endure a less severe kind of illness than Palmer's. Feeling like hell in the middle of the night can do remarkable things for my prayer life as I call to mind how good I used to feel and hope to feel that way again soon. I feel needy at those times, and I want God to get busy doing something to help. In many of the psalms, David is clearly suffering, and he doesn't hold back letting God know about it. But in the "watches of the night," he comforts himself in the knowledge that, even if not spared from suffering and darkness, God will sustain him through those times: "I will call to mind the deeds of the Lord; I will remember your wonders of old" (Ps 77:11); "Bless the Lord, O my soul, and do not forget all his benefits" (Ps 103:2).

One day not long ago, I did feel like hell in the middle of the night and just as bad when I woke up. I was dizzy getting out of bed, and it took me a while to pull myself together to go to work. A few days later the feeling hit me so badly it drove me to bed with my head ringing and my body unable to move. My doctor said I had a viral infection in my inner ear that would take time to heal. In the meantime, I had to suffer thorough it. This wasn't what I wanted to hear. The Internet is often a scary place for finding out more about what ails you (clicking enough links always seems to lead to CANCER!), and I read reports of awful diseases like Meniere's, which robs the victim of balance and turns the world into a spinning room. Through the inner ear, the body gets a sense of itself as a physical object moving through the world. I never realized the importance of that structure to my sense of balance and ability to orient myself, but also to my sense of well-being. I appreciate it so much better now. I wanted quick medical action, a speedy cure for my suffering, but my ear, nose, and throat specialist wasn't much help, other than to assure me I would probably live through it (he took this way too lightly).

Every so often for several months, I experienced a terrible sense of being an extra step removed from my extremities, less stable on my feet, and I endured an odd combination of disorientation, tension, malaise, and anxiety. During those moments, the universe wasn't a friendly place, and I felt my vulnerability more keenly—and the inability of anyone to do much to help. Boundaries of self seemed to close in on me, while I waited for the clouds to lift. Even several months later, with the healing on track, I still was occasionally revisited by symptoms transmuted into something hard to describe: a sense of dread and apprehension, a "troubled spirit."

At some point during that time, I planned to go abroad for a professional opportunity, accepting an invitation from colleagues at a university in Spain who wanted me to come for a week to teach a class. I've logged my share of miles and spent a lot of time in airports and hotels, but I'm not at the "road warrior" stage where traveling becomes drudgery. It still has an element of adventure for me, which usually makes me look forward to it. International opportunities are even better, and this was the kind of opportunity I've always jumped at. I'd been to that university a couple of times before, but I didn't feel as up to it this time. My troubled spirit returned that week, and I felt uneasy at the idea of being away—at the prospect of a double dislocation from health and home, away from family and familiar routines. I felt like I did when I started going camping as a Boy Scout and had to pack for a trip the next day. Unlike the kid-friendly group my boys joined, Troop 5 back in Tennessee was a tough-love outfit, and if you didn't get it together before you left, you would be cold and eating stale Pop Tarts in the dark. Standing in the garage of my family's home the night before, trying to find my scattered gear, I sometimes felt a chill of apprehension, knowing it was up to me to get it together, and it made my warm bed at home much more attractive.

Sometimes I get that same twinge of apprehension mingled with excitement before taking a long trip. Overseas journeys add another level of preparation with uncertainties about what to expect and what to bring. A troubled spirit doesn't help. My malaise shifted my frame of mind and accentuated the feeling that to be away from the familiar, to be overseas in a strange place, meant an unwelcome, heightened sense of risk and being alone. I'm used to traveling alone, but this was more of an existential loneliness. My own body felt a bit unfriendly, as did the universe, so venturing into the wide world didn't seem appealing. I needed to pack and get organized, to go through my long checklist of things to bring, but also to prepare myself, to get my head on straight and strengthen my spirit.

This kind of trip is often stressful and requires a willingness to accept a level of uncertainty, especially if I'm called to lecture or teach. I'm not always sure what will happen or what I'm supposed to say, and the expectations of my hosts are not always clear, but I keep pushing myself to go for it, do my best to prepare, and "let go." In that sense, these experiences resemble the initiation rites in many societies that Richard Rohr argues are valuable for leading new members out of business as usual and into "limnal," or threshold, space where they can learn. In his book *Everything Belongs*, he crystallizes an important aspect of these rites that seems just as relevant to the international journey: "voluntary displacement for the sake of transformation."[3]

The voluntary displacement, which when I'm healthy stimulates and excites me, takes on a different cast under conditions of illness and greater vulnerability. It's hard to let go when you feel small, when you'd rather stay home with the familiar than go away to the novel and strange, when you feel like hell and simply want it to end. At home it was cold, windy, and raining, and my physical sensations told me to hunker down. But that wasn't possible, and, besides, I'm called to step out in faith in spite of those feelings. I need to trust that God will enable me when I'm called to grow and would rather stay where I am, when I feel like hell and need to remember how I used to feel and trust that I'll feel that way again. If I do that, God goes to work in my life to drive me to a deeper intimacy, allowing me not only to carry on but to grow stronger.

On the way to Spain, I had a lot of time to reflect on the existential loneliness of the long-distance and sometimes ailing academic. Many go to great lengths to avoid that feeling, staying connected to home with cell phones and laptops. I often get restless in a hotel room and want to find something to do, and the distractions of the nightlife beckon. But I also like the opportunity of solitude that being alone provides. When I'm by myself and away from home, more aware of the boundaries of my solitude within the travel "bubble," I have a better awareness of an inner conversation. I don't sleep much on those long flights, so I do a lot of thinking. I needed to let go of my concern that I wouldn't be all right physically, to know that God does not go away in between the times when I feel good, that suffering is a hard reality where God is felt even more keenly, that I have a place to stand where I am safe. I needed to trust that no matter where I am in the world, I am safe within my inner spirit that is part of a larger sacred world of spirit. I can often feel this world more strongly when I travel in solitude. God's love chases after me, draws me inward, and his hand presses me down toward that "firm foundation" where I won't fall, even if I feel dizzy and off balance. The God of Psalms is a fortress, a strong and mighty rock. The Christian tradition uses the same language, as in the old hymn I love: "On Christ the solid rock I stand."

Staying home is simpler, but the borders of my world shrink in on themselves if I don't keep pushing them out. At my stage of life, there's always the temptation to play it safe, to consolidate my gains. But we're called to grow and continually be in the process of transformation. In spiritual terms, we're called to "repentance," not as a single moment of decision but as an ongoing willingness to "turn" and see things anew, to live continually in the process of self-examination. Traveling far from home helps me do that. It's a way for me to grow and to participate in a wider community. Travelers today often try to control the environment by bringing "home" along with them, going with a familiar group, eating recognizable fast food. We can buy the experiences with which we feel most comfortable, and globalized business provides the same familiar places to stay: the Hiltons, Hyatts, and Sheratons. But in earlier times, the disciples counted on little else than hospitality in following Jesus' instructions: "Take nothing for the journey—no staff, no bag, no bread, no money, no extra tunic" (Luke 9:3). By necessity, that forced them into people's homes and into relationships. Through the hospitality of many colleagues, my web of relationships has grown, and so have the world and the community in which I live. I know from experience that I can count on amazing kindness and grace. I can (and often must) throw myself on the hospitality of others, as they can throw themselves on mine.

After a week's teaching and a warm reunion with colleagues and old friends, and getting to know new ones, I headed home from Spain. My thoughts were full of pleasant memories of that visit and visits from years past. I felt I had grown again, and my scope extended a little broader. As I rode in the taxi from the hotel to the Madrid airport on a sunny Saturday morning for the flight back to the States, I felt rested and relaxed. My troubled spirit was banished for the moment, and I looked forward to home and family. In the absence of malaise, I felt almost euphoric. But then, being alive should feel like that more often—if we are mindful enough to notice and appreciate it. David had this kind of mindfulness when he said, "I will yet praise him." He knew how it felt to suffer, but also knew how rich life had been, is, and will be: "my cup overflows."

The end of my life may come more abruptly, but if illness strikes and there is no getting better, I hope I am faithful enough to trust that, if not a cure, at least a greater healing awaits. The dislocation and involuntary vulnerability of illness can make us more available to transformation, to seeking and experiencing the divine presence that we all have in common. Going inward takes me "outward" into a greater sense of community, and that leads me to feel more spiritually at home wherever I am. We cannot flee from God's spirit, even on the "far side of the sea." We have a safe place to stand wherever we are and however we feel.

Notes

1. Richard Rohr, *Men and Women: The Journey of Spiritual Transformation* (St. Anthony Messenger Press, 1999) CD collection.

2. Parker Palmer, *Let your Life Speak: Listening for the Voice of Vocation* (San Francisco: Jossey-Bass, 2000).

3. Richard Rohr, *Everything Belongs* (New York: Crossroad Pub., 2003) 19.

Chapter 16

FAITH VERTIGO

For my thoughts are not your thoughts, neither are your ways my ways, declares the Lord. (Isaiah 55:8-9)

Faith is an ongoing process of figuring out who we are in relationship to God. But for me, that relationship easily gets wrapped up in my sense of God doing something to me or for me, or wishing God would: thank you for this, thank you for that, or maybe "God, I wish you hadn't done that." Simply acknowledging who God is and praising God for that, which seems so basic to faith, doesn't always come easily to my American Protestant strand of Christianity. I don't always know how best to praise God, except to be grateful for what I appreciate about my life. Praising and thanking get mixed together. But before I get around to thanking, I've got to get something else straight. The flip side of becoming vulnerable and available for the grace of God is elevating the place of God—just like the children's song I learned a long time ago: "They [we] are weak, but he is strong."[1] I must recognize that God's ways are not my ways, and I'll never know what God knows. I like the way Isaiah captures this relationship: "'For my thoughts are not your thoughts, neither are your ways my ways,' declares the LORD. 'As the heavens are higher than the earth, so are my ways higher than your ways and my thoughts than your thoughts'" (Isa 55:8-9).

My incomplete conception of God has to make room for mystery. As David says in Psalm 139, "Such knowledge is too wonderful for me; it is so high that I cannot attain it." That's a good thing. I would hate to limit God to my conception, or to have what God does depend on me.

I am taught to praise God for being "faithful." I'm not always sure what that means, but I think it's not so much that I should believe in God but that God believes in me, that God is with me. I'm not alone. That truth has difficulty competing against other more instant-gratification, self-centered beliefs: that if I believe in God—that is, to the extent that I myself am faithful to God—I'll get to live forever, or I'll at least be rich until then. I like believing that. But my own faithfulness hangs by a thread, easily disturbed by whatever frightens, distracts, or bothers me at any given time. I suppose that's why the prophets spent so much of their time trying to explain this simple principle: God is faithful, even when we're not (which is a lot of the time).

This is a good place to start. Isaiah also has God saying, "Don't fear, for I am with you." How's that supposed to make me feel better? I don't know, but it does. Job, at the end of his season of suffering, said, "Okay, God, I get it. I don't understand a lot of things that are too wonderful for me, but I'm all right because I feel like I can *see* you, I can *see* what before I guess I had only *heard* about." He finally understood who God was, and who Job was in relation to God—that is, Job was perfectly not God but perfectly God's. God becomes God to me when I accept the truth of Isaiah's words, that God's thoughts are not my thoughts. When I submit to God, I accept that only in my weakness can God be for me who God is and do for me what God wants to do. I can accept that God has something good in mind for us, maybe not good as we define it, but we can trust that it will be good in God's way that only God knows. As is said through Jeremiah, "Surely I know the plans I have for you, plans for good and not for evil" (Jer 29:11).

One day shortly after work, I got a phone call from my wife. She said she had received a troubling call from the high school, where my younger son was starting his senior year. One of the school counselors said a teacher told her that Daniel supposedly expressed to another student that he planned to kill himself over the weekend. An awful feeling of dread, fear, and disbelief hit me when I heard the news. Carol said she was on her way to find out more, and I stopped what I was doing and headed to join her. As I walked to the car, my mind reeled with questions about what could possibly be going on with my son, the wonderful young man with the easygoing, gentle spirit who was always upbeat, smiling, and thinking of others. I thought of how much he meant to me, how much I enjoyed being with him.

I knew he had been working hard at school, staying up late, trying to find time to get everything done. He was determined to do well in school, and Carol and I were both incredibly proud of him. I know teenagers struggle with issues of having friends, of self-worth, of finding their identity. Seniors face a special challenge, with the pressures for success, wondering about future career plans, and the work that goes into college applications. Could the pressure have mounted up enough to cause thoughts of suicide? I can't possibly know everything that goes on in the lives of my children, but I didn't think I was *that* out of touch.

The idea of my son being brought to such a point of despair was tough to consider. It broke my heart to picture his smiling face while trying to comprehend what awful possibilities might lie beneath the surface. As I drove to the high school, I considered the possibility that the lives of my family could be changed forever. Life had seemed so normal just a few minutes earlier. I had looked forward to the weekend and to my usual routine after a busy week, maybe watching the school's football game that night. On one hand, I still couldn't imagine that it was possible. But now I tried to recall anything Daniel might have said over the last several months—any clues at all. He had not seemed depressed and hadn't been preoccupied with dark thoughts or withdrawn from friends and family—none of the warning signs I thought I knew. I thought we communicated well. Wouldn't he have come to one of us if he were that burdened? On the other hand, what if it were true? Maybe we had been oblivious to his life and fooling ourselves that everything was all right. I remembered parents who always seemed to say after such a tragedy, "He seemed like he was doing fine; we never suspected anything was wrong." I didn't want to be one of them.

When I arrived, I found Carol already speaking with the school counselor and piecing together the story. That morning, a student confided in a teacher that another girl had told her a boy, identified as our son, supposedly said he planned to kill himself over the weekend and wondered what it would feel like. The teacher then notified the counseling office, and Daniel was called in. He denied knowing anything about the conversation and said he had no idea what they were talking about. These days, teachers are encouraged to report anything that might mean a student is at risk, so the teacher followed procedure. But in keeping the student's confidence, she wouldn't say who told her about Daniel, which meant we couldn't get to the bottom of the situation. Also, it was late on a Friday afternoon, so we could learn nothing else until the next week. We were simply left to deal with the information. The counselor, with little more to add, said to keep an eye on

Daniel, making the weekend loom as a potential time of danger and uncertainty.

Daniel was still at the school in the newspaper office, where he worked as photo editor, and we were eager to see him. He was standing in the hall when we got there, and he gave us a big smile and hug. He seemed his usual self, and that was a relief. Just to see him and put my arms around him was reassuring. And yet the seed had been planted. Was he just trying to cover up and reassure us that everything was all right? I wished I could go back to my life a few hours before and reclaim my peace of mind. He was staying at school to take shots of the game, but I didn't feel much like football.

I wondered what I should do when we all got home. Daniel didn't want to talk about it anymore, and I understood that. He was accused of something, and I'm sure it embarrassed him. Teenagers don't appreciate unwanted attention, much less from their parents. I gave him an extra hug that night before bed and let it go, but something needed to be expressed, and we needed closure. I wanted to be careful to find the right words, and I hoped God would give them to me.

Faithfulness has something to do with trust. In moments of doubt, I hear God asking me, "Don't you trust me? Haven't I been with you so far? Look how I've worked in your life." God is faithful even when I'm not. Having that reassurance strengthens my ability to trust that he is working out a plan in my life—a good plan. That idea also helps me be a dad. Just as God is faithful toward me, I need to have faith in my children, to know them and to believe in them. My faith in my children can't be based only on their accomplishments. I am proud of what they do, but even if they don't always do praiseworthy things, I want to be faithful toward them.

The thought of my son attempting to end his life shook me to the core. I kept remembering the cold chill when I first heard the news from school. Neither my wife nor I wanted to be in denial, to ignore something that needed addressing. Did I really know Daniel the way I thought I did? What had been going on all these years that I was unaware of? That year was busy for all of us, and I hadn't been able to spend nearly as much time with my son as I wished. What kind of hidden life had grown up while I wasn't around? I had tried to plant seeds of a faith discipline in both of my sons. I encourage them not to be anxious about the future but thankful for each day and to watch how the special gifts of life unfold in front of them. I know people can get depressed and can't see their way clear, but the idea of suicide is completely contrary to the attitude of obedient hope. I couldn't bring myself to imagine that Daniel had considered it. But no matter what I feared might be the case, I had to have faith in my son, to trust that God was working for something good in his life. My faith in Daniel could not depend on something he did or did not do, or something I thought he might do.

The next night, when we had dinner together, I told Daniel I wanted to say a few words that he needed to hear, and then we didn't need to talk about it anymore. I said, "We believe you, and we believe *in* you. We've loved you your whole life, and we have faith that we know you, the real you." (I guess that's pretty much what we want God to say to us.) Finally, I said, "We trust that God is involved in your life and leading you in the right direction. We know God has something wonderful in mind for you, and as your parents we're excited to see what life holds in store."

It proved to be a case of mistaken identity. Third-hand reports produced details that didn't fit our son, including a conversation he denied having. A new counselor who didn't know our son had passed on information from a teacher who also didn't know him. But in erring on the side of caution and confidentiality, the school for a time had brought an unwelcome and unknown accusing visitor into our home. We wondered how far the rumor spread, but in the end we encouraged Daniel to be himself, the self that we all knew and respected, and the rest would resolve itself. And it has.

A few months later, my son and I went camping at the Big Bend National Park. It's a wild, isolated part of southwestern Texas, a desert region with rugged mountains and rocky trails. Daniel has become a skilled photographer, and I looked forward to having time together and watching him work in such a picturesque place. Along with some of his friends, we hiked up a particularly tall peak one cold, sunny morning in early January. It took most of the morning to reach the top, where we could see the valley stretched out below and look out toward distant peaks beyond into Mexico. As the temperature climbed, I could smell the pitch in the pine trees heating up, and the wind whipped over the ridge of the mountain where we stopped and found a place to eat lunch. One craggy cliff provided a spectacular view of the desert floor, a sheer drop-off, so of course the fearless teens climbed out on it and sat with their legs dangling over the edge into the abyss.

Parenting gives you an awful feeling of responsibility for your kids when you think they may be in danger. You want to protect them from anything that might hurt them, but of course you can't always do that. As Daniel swapped one camera lens for another and shot away, I pleaded with him to inch back from the edge so my nerves could get some relief. Why are such moments so unnerving? My son is an extension of me, he's part of me, and yet I'm not in control of what he does—at least now that he's not a kid anymore. (I already figured that out from my first son.) Watching him, I experienced vertigo without the control that comes with being able to step back from the edge whenever I want.

But we have to let them go into whatever future God has for them. I need to have faith in them—not that I always approve of what they do (although I would like to), but I must believe in them. I have to let myself go into that future too. I praise God for being faithful, knowing I can trust God with my life and with the lives of my children and loved ones. God is with us, and we're not alone, and sometimes, when I stand on the mountain and look out on the valley below, I can see a little bit of God and can hear that voice saying, "Don't you trust me?" That's enough for now. I'm reminded once again that God is faithful even when I'm not, that God's ways are not my ways and God's thoughts not my thoughts. And I can praise God for that.

Note

1. "Jesus Loves Me," words by Anna B. Warner (1860), music by William B. Bradbury (1862).

AFTERWORD

The thinking Christian has a place in the community of faith. We can have a deep and passionate experience of God while resisting the limits of fundamentalism. The faith journey leads not only to abstract theological principles, but it leads through them to the lived experience of everyday life. In the crucial spiritual paradox that welcomes us into the experience of grace, God's power is made perfect in weakness. Without claiming any kind of moral superiority or theological mastery, I have tried to show, through examples from my own life, how God can work powerfully through us to the extent that we are able to submit to God, to set aside the things within ourselves that hinder that power—to become "weak." Men find this especially difficult, but all of us face the struggle in our own ways. Whether with religion or any other subject, we are conditioned to believe that greater learning and understanding lead progressively to greater certainty—about our own correctness and the wrongness of those who disagree with us. God becomes another of our opinions, and much of current religious culture fuels that conviction of certitude. In her book, *Plan B: Further Thoughts on Faith*, Anne Lamott describes a friend with a fatal illness who needed a spiritual connection but wasn't getting one. She sought out Lamott, who described the situation this way:

> After various people at her church kept saying that she should be happy—she was going home to be with Jesus. This is the type of thing that gives Christians a bad name. This and the Inquisition. Some of her evangelical friends had insisted sorrowfully that her nieces wouldn't get into heaven, since they were Jews, as was one of her sisters.[1]

People like that have been part of the Bible-belt landscape of my life, but that's not the kind of Jesus company I keep. In the wonderful documentary *Nobelity*, featuring interviews with a number of Nobel Prize winners, Bishop Desmond Tutu explains the importance of openness toward the beliefs of others—that God sees things more inclusively than we ever can. "God is not a Christian," he said.[2] I agree, and yet I find my home in the Christian tradition. That's where my authentic experience lies, so within that tradition I join with others in seeking a connection with the larger mysteries. In the paradoxical realm of the spirit, greater learning and awareness invite certainty to yield to greater openness. Getting serious about faith means being thoughtful but not over-intellectualizing the journey. There's a rich interplay between mind and heart that leads us ever deeper in the mysteries of faith and closer to God. The lengthy, logical arguments of the Apostle Paul himself, from whom I draw so much of my theme, finally give way in one of his letters to a doxological outburst of praise: "O the depth of the riches and wisdom and knowledge of God! How unsearchable are his judgments and how inscrutable his ways!" (Rom 1:33).

I'm sure I'm not the only kid who began to wonder with puzzlement what I would find if I traveled to the known limits of the universe and then kept going. What's beyond that? Imagining myself traveling backwards in infinite time stimulated a similarly befuddling question: "How did God get there in the first place?" I even got an oddly palpable and slightly unpleasant feeling of bewilderment when I contemplated those unanswerables. We soon realize that we can never overcome our inadequacy before such questions. When we reach adulthood, if we continue to think about such things, we may choose simply to be intentionally aware of the "unanswerables" with a more mature spirit. John Berryman's poem, "Address to the Lord," gives me that sense of awareness.

> Whatever your end may be, accept my amazement.
> May I stand until death forever at attention
> for any your least instruction or enlightenment.
> I even feel sure you will assist me again, Master of insight & beauty[3]

Out of that wonder and awareness of our own weakness, we are able to take a leap of faith and draw upon greater strengths for daily living. From this perspective and as a final prayerful note, I can express in my own words a confession to my Master:

In my wandering, find me,
In my inadequacy, receive me,
In my brokenness, mend me,
In my woundedness, heal me,
In my emptiness, fill me,
In my hunger, feed me,
In my dullness, sharpen me,
In my restlessness, calm me,
In my anxiety, embolden me,
In my yearning, satisfy me,
In my smallness, grow me,
In my weakness, strengthen me,
And in my abundance, put me to work.

Amen.

Notes

1. Anne Lamott, *Plan B: Further Thoughts on Faith* (New York: Riverhead Books, 2005) 269.

2. *Nobelity*, written and dir. Turk Pipkin, 501audio, 2006.

3. John Berryman, *John Berryman Collected Poems 1937-1971* (New York: Farrar, Straus & Giroux, 1989) 215.

EPILOGUE

The personal journey I plot here reflects an even larger conversation, a religious transformation at work in the world. I share this journey with other thoughtful believers as we experience something radically new in the world of faith. But because we live in the middle of it, we can't easily see what's happening or find words to describe it. I've tried to show how I've experienced this transformation from inside a life looking out, wrestling with the stirrings in my own spirit, with a restlessness not easy to name in this post-denominational world. Like many others, I've lived it without knowing it.

Not yet fully clear in form, this upheaval has been called the "Great Emergence," or the emerging church, a movement to which existing religious institutions must adapt. Indeed, some see this reconfiguring of religious life as the biggest shakeup since the Protestant Reformation. In her book, *The Great Emergence: How Christianity Is Changing and Why*, Phyllis Tickle distinguishes among four key Christian traditions in the "quadrilateral": the "liturgicals" (Catholic, Anglican); "social justice Christians" (mainline Protestant); "renewalists" (charismatic, Pentecostal); and "conservatives" (evangelicals).[1] Beyond the polarizations that have divided these groups from each other and from secular society, Emergent Christians find themselves in a "gathering center," looking for a new way to "do church" that resides in a conversation taking place within and across these traditions.

In its gathering, the movement tracks the same disintegration and reconstitution occurring with other institutions, as people reject the authority of hierarchical organizations to seek their own forms of authentic engagement in more fluid communities that don't track traditional formal boundaries—a kind of Religion 2.0. At the margins and intersections of these diverse, reconfiguring communities—where I find myself—lie exciting and energizing possibilities for believers.

I see these emergent ideas in my experience, and that lets me take something sociological—trends in the abstract and often not easy to describe—and see through it to real life: mine and yours. In working through my spiritual formation, through these devotional reflections wrapped in a broader conversation, I find myself trying to answer the same central question driving the great emergence: "How can we live responsibly as devout and faithful adherents of one religion in a world of many religions?"[2] In its post-evangelical and postmodern character, emergent theology swaps an exclusionary in-or-out mentality for a conversation about the Truth.

I can relate to those ideas. I suppose my "emergent"-friendly faith and writing flow naturally from my experiences as a global citizen and educator. I'm unlikely to mindlessly accept hierarchically based truth claims, a rigid fundamentalism, or literal authority. Like the emergents, I am less apt to approach Scripture as ultimate authority that contains historically correct news accounts; instead, I regard it as an inspired narrative of God's redemptive actions. I seek meaning in community with others, in relationships with diverse companions—whether my Jewish spouse, my evangelical friends, or secular colleagues. I find myself drawn to diverse sources—from the lowbrow televangelists to the serious scholars.

As the emergent conversation grows, more people will seek guides, resources, and reflections told from a perspective they find familiar and from someone they recognize. As a writer approaching faith, not as a religious professional but as a seeker, I offer these reflections to others who find their way toward the gathering center.

Notes

1. Phyllis Tickle, *The Great Emergence: How Christianity Is Changing and Why* (Grand Rapids MI: Baker Books, 2008).

2. Ibid., 73.